Aut ry

Cold Porcelain and Sugar Flowers

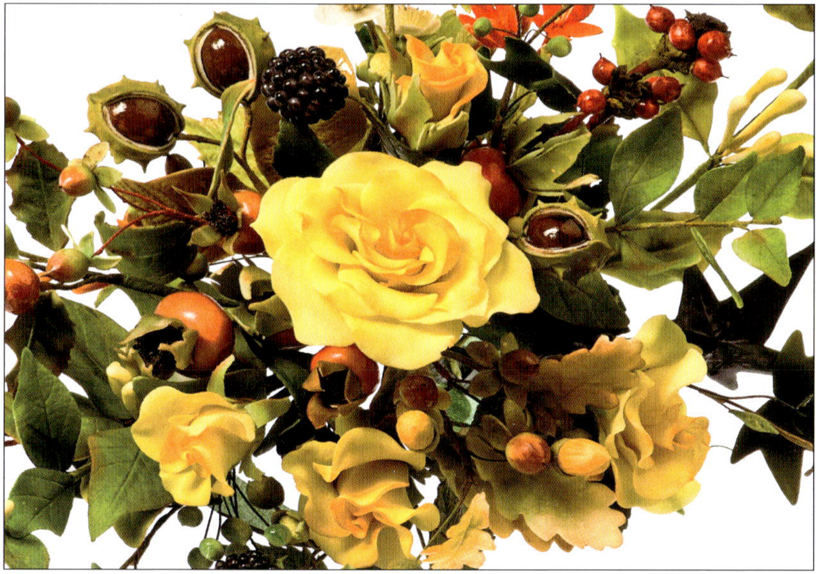

As Summer draws to a close and the days grow cool, the emptiness of the fading flowers is quickly replaced by the warmth of the colours created by the seeds, berries and fruits that they leave behind. An explosion of reds, oranges, yellows and browns fill the garden with a new lease of life and gives comfort in the knowledge that in just a few months, it will all bloom again.

By Alyson Reynolds

First Edition – March 2012

Published by A M Reynolds Publishing

The Yews, Lein Road, Kingston on Spey
Fochabers, Moray, IV32 7NW

ISBN 978-0-9571554-0-4

A catalogue record for this book is available from the British Library.

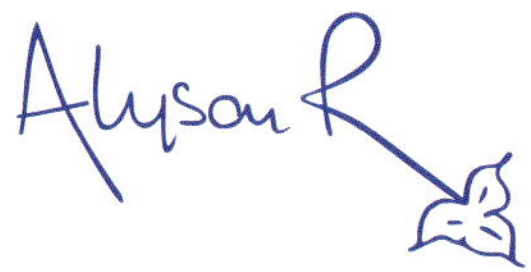

Written & Designed by Alyson Reynolds

Design & Layout by Andrew Gransden © 2012

Photography by Andrew Gransden Photography © 2012

Drawings by Alyson Reynolds © 2012

Printed and Bound by MMS Almac Ltd, Elgin, Moray, IV30 1XY

Dedicated to

My sons Peter and Felix & my sisters Jacki and Clare

With love and chuckles x

They say that you can't choose your family, but you can choose your friends. I am fortunate to know that my family are among my friends and my friends are my extended family.

All drawings, handcrafted flowers and arrangements contained within this book have been made by Alyson Reynolds

Contents

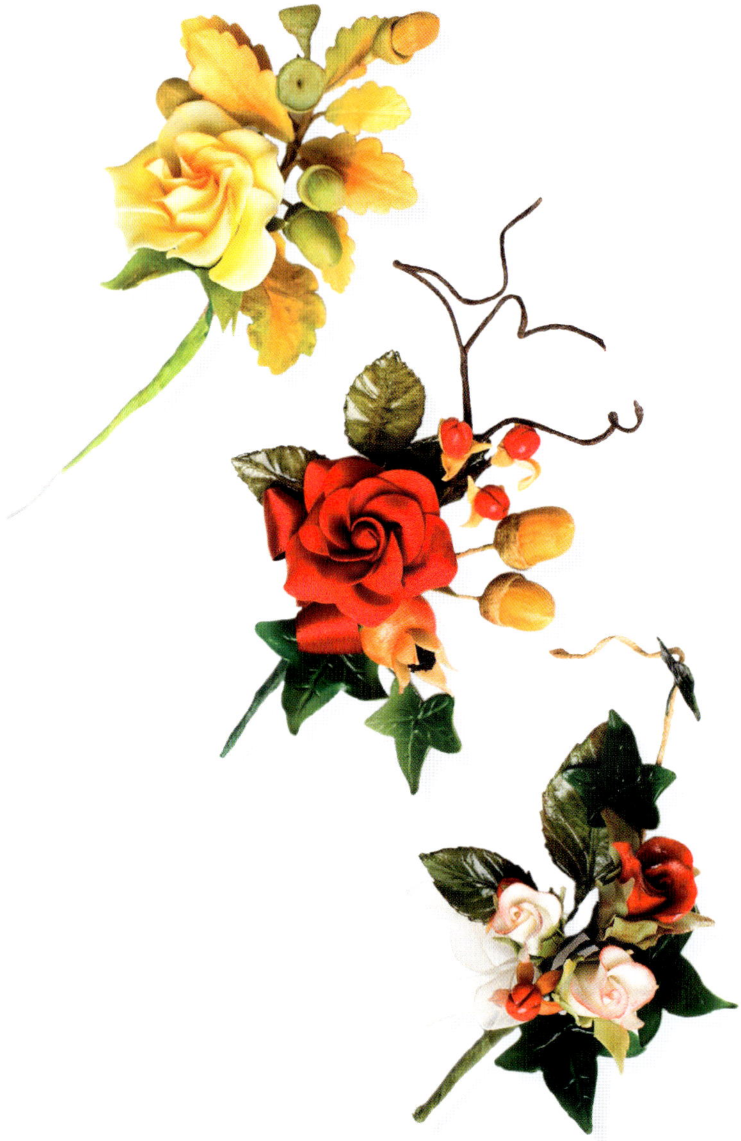

Foreword

I first met Alyson some years ago at Squires Kitchen in Farnham, and since then have been continually amazed by her creativity and natural ability for making lifelike flowers and arrangements without the need for everything to be botanically perfect. Her talents extend to teaching this amazing skill, and it has been a great pleasure for me and my students at Tårtdecor, Sweden to have enjoyed her company on many occasions.

Alyson is very popular with all students. She inspires them to enjoy themselves and to discover the pleasure of making flowers along with bringing out their own creative flair. Her encouragement gives students confidence in what they do and motivates them to think independently, using instructions as a guide rather than the rule. An example of this is with regard to the colour palettes in this book; she proposes that you use base colours – perhaps already in your 'tool box', and to experiment with mixing them together to reveal many variations and shades. Read this book with confidence and allow yourself to become inspired and discover this pleasurable art.

Over time, Alyson has become one of my very best 'sugarcraft-friends'. It has been lovely getting to know her and her charming sons, Peter and Felix, who have supported their Mother in every moment. I feel very honoured to be asked to write the foreword to this book and I wish you all the best Alyson.

With Love

Agneta Olsson

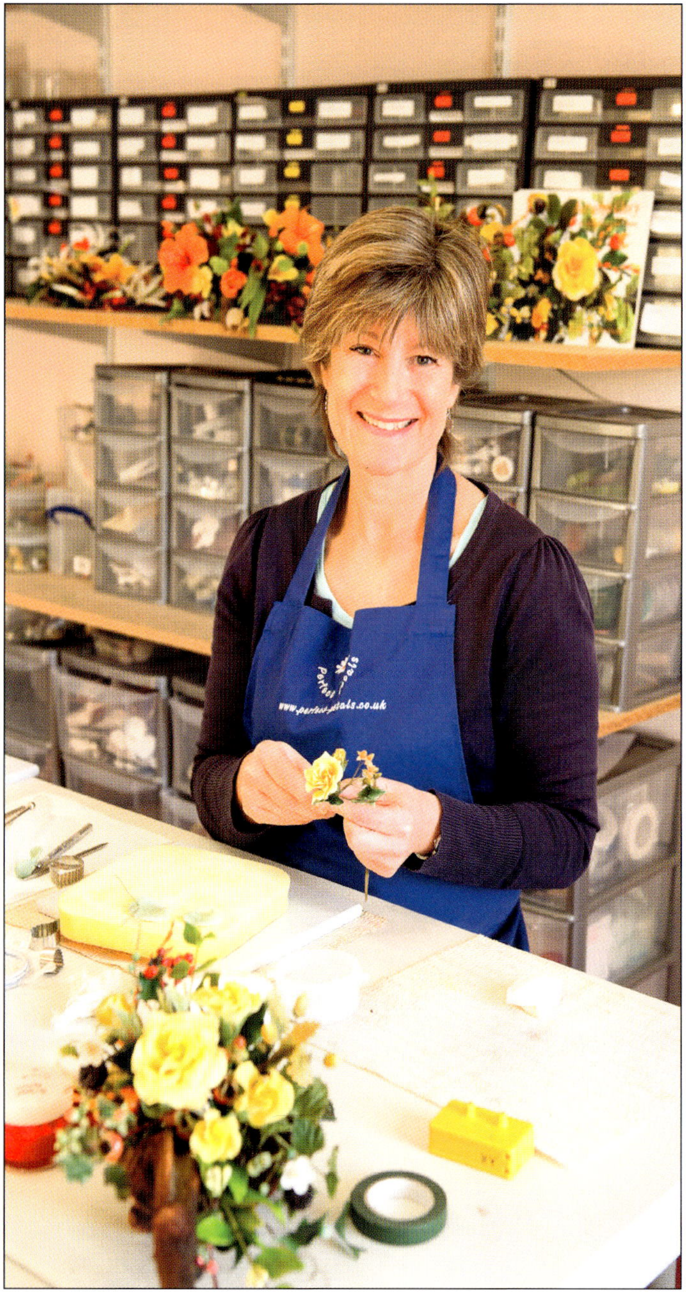

In my workroom

An introduction to this book

On the morning I awoke to find my fingers replaced by sausages and my car keys in the fridge, my lovely niece Katie announced that she had decided to embrace her hips and that I should embrace my curves. I pondered on this statement for a while before it dawned on me too, that perhaps it was time to 'embrace my curves'.

You may be wondering what on earth this has to do with making cold porcelain and sugar flowers, but it was those words that prompted me to take stock and to recognise the things that I can do, to value my gifts (whatever they may be) and to use my knowledge as a foundation for inspiration. And so, through this book I hope to use this theme to encourage you to explore the creativity that lies within you....

From scribble pads to Rembrandt we all have our own style and that is what makes each of us original. This book will not dot i's and cross t's – it lies outside the confines of restrictions and simply teaches you to do as you please, with a little guidance.

If you are new to this craft, be assured, everything in this book is within your capability. My aim is to share my knowledge and to demonstrate what can be achieved with the minimum of fuss. For those of you with experience, I believe there is always something more to learn. Within the pages there are photographs suggesting ways of how you can develop and show off your skills, be it a sugar decoration for a cake or a cold porcelain table setting. All the photographs have been taken on a white background so there is no influence of colour other than that which has been applied directly to the flowers. What you see is what you get – warts and all.

Autumn Glory is made up from a compilation of 9 individual 'Stories'. Each Story is capable of standing alone but when joined together as chapters in a book they become a novel - and you will be writing the ending. Here is a project to bring pleasure and to enjoy with no pressure, just let it all happen and ....

Embrace your curves ...

Getting started

All flowers are simple if you take a moment to break them down and build them up, one step at a time.

There are only two main differences in making flowers from sugar and making them from cold porcelain. Firstly, sugar is edible and cold porcelain is not. Secondly cold porcelain is far more durable and less susceptible to the elements of light, heat and water. It will last a lot longer.

I have listed equipment to guide you for this project. There is no requirement for you to use the same to achieve great results. Look at what you have in your tool box if you have one. All the same tools, cutters, colours and veiners can be used for both sugar and cold porcelain. Cutters and veiners can be used in several ways to create different leaves and petals. If you don't have a workable cutter just go for it, step into the garden and pick a petal or two then you can cut and vein the shapes by hand.

Types of cold porcelain

There are several types of Cold Porcelain and modelling clay on the market now – many of which are air drying. Some are very lightweight. You could try Craft Porcelain Fria or Modena Modelling Clay OR why not make you own from a very simple recipe below. Go on give it a go ... it's not rocket science!

- 1 cup wood glue - made from half cup liberon super wood glue and half cup normal PVA such as Impex Hi-tack craft glue
- 1 cup good quality cornflour
- 1 - 2 tablespoons baby oil

Put oil and glue in a NON-STICK saucepan and mix together with a wooden spoon. Stir in the cup of cornflour and mix it well in. Place over a low heat stirring constantly until like choux pastry it gathers around the spoon. It will get lumpy at first but keep going. When it rolls into a ball without sticking to your hands it's ready.

Take off the heat and gently knead to clear any big lumps. Be careful not to knead too long or you will toughen the paste. You can use this straight away or wrap in cling film and keep in an airtight container.

Materials - for this project

- Cold porcelain or sugar flower/petal paste
- Florist tape - nile green, moss green, red and beige
- Wires - 18, 20, 22, 24, 26, 28 & 30g (gauge) green and 24 & 26g white
- Cotton thread - burgundy, cream, pale yellow and white
- Stamens - white seedhead small
- Fine semolina to make your own pollen (see Page 13)
- Confectioners varnish and PME edible glaze (for sugar)
- Matt sealing spray or hairspray (cold porcelain)
- Colour dusts – see colour palettes on Page 12
- Colour pastes – pale green, purple, pale yellow and cream

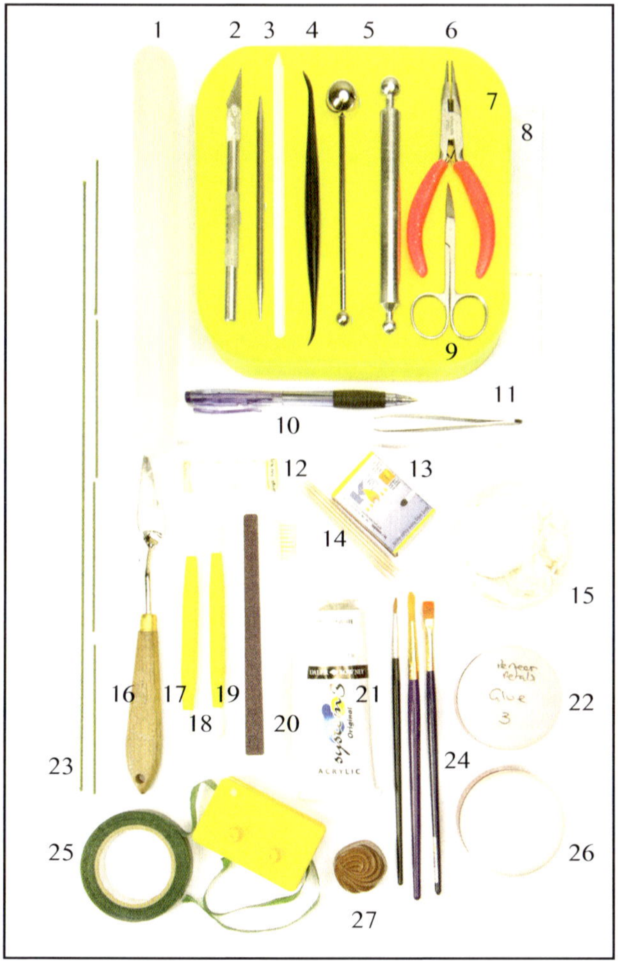

Tool Box - useful to have.

1 Non stick rolling pin
2 Scalpel
3 Cel sticks (metal or plastic)
4 Veining tool
5 Ball tools
6 Pliers
7 Cel Pad
8 Non-stick board - grooved on one side can be helpful
9 Scissors
10 Pen or pencil
11 Tweezers
12 Cotton thread
13 Matches
14 Cocktail sticks
15 Cornflour
16 Palette knife
17 Cutting wheel
18 Arrowhead tool
19 Emery board
20 Small toothbrush
21 White gouache, oil or acrylic paint (cold porcelain)
22 Glue (PVA for cold porcelain or edible glue for sugar)
23 Florist wire
24 Artists brushes
25 Florist tape cutter – cuts tape into ½ and ¼ width
26 Cream moisturiser (CP) or White Vegetable Fat (Sugar) - to prevent paste sticking to board
27 Chocolates – for the artist – most important.

Cutters and Veiners - for this project

- Rose petal cutters and veiner – I use the veins on my hands.
- Calyx cutters (small for hypericum berries/blackberries and larger/medium for roses and rosehips)
- Metal leaf cutters 25-55mm (for honeysuckle and hypericum leaves)
- Honeysuckle leaf veiner
- Black Bryony leaf veiner (used for hypericum leaf)
- Rose leaf cutters for rose and blackberry leaves
- Rose leaf veiners
- Oak leaf cutters and veiner
- Ivy cutters and veiner
- 5 petal blossom cutter for blackberry flower
- Blackberry leaf veiner
- Horse Chestnut leaf veiner

See Pages 70-73 for details of cutters and veiners used in this book.

Tips and techniques

Tools

Of all the tools the 3 most useful are the ball tool, the scalpel and the cel stick. Keep these 3 clean and blades sharp and you can't go wrong. If you find paste sticking to the ball tool, dust it with cornflour. If you have dried paste on the ball tool it will stick to and tear the petals you are working on. Metal tools tend to work better with cold porcelain than plastic ones as the cold metal helps to prevent the paste from sticking.

To get a good curl along the edge of the a petal or leaf, dab a little cornflour onto the paste, hold the ball tool as you would a pencil, place the ball half on and half off the edge of the paste near the bottom and gently push with a smooth continuous motion completely around the whole shape. Dust off the excess cornflour. To get a gentle cupped effect, place the ball tool just inside but away from the edge of the petal push or roll around the shape as above. For a truly cupped petal, place the ball tool in the centre of the petal and make small circular motions which will curl up the sides.

Wires and florist tape

In general cut your wires longer rather than shorter as it is easier to cut them off than it is to add them on.

Gently pull the florist tape to release the gum whilst wrapping tightly down and around the stem. See link on www.alyson-reynolds.com for visual reference.

Cutters and Veiners

All types of cutters can be used with both sugar and cold porcelain, however in general, I find that when using cold porcelain, metal cutters give a cleaner cut and don't clog as much as plastic.

If paste is sticking to the cutter, rub a little cold cream or lard around the edge of the cutter before use, OR lightly dust cornflour onto the paste before cutting out.

Keep all cutters clean - they will cut better and last longer.

Wash veiners with warm soapy water before use to avoid contaminating white paste with rogue colour. Even the smallest spot of colour dust, particularly red, will bleed into the paste and the tiny dot will turn into an ugly spot.

For Cold Porcelain

Always add white oil paint, acrylic or gouache to paste before using. This prevents paste appearing opaque when dry.

Add base colour to paste AFTER oil/gouache/acrylic has been added to ensure you get a true colour representation.

Remember shrinkage. Cold porcelain shrinks as it dries and therefore allowances need to be made, otherwise the beautiful bloom you made the night before may become a shadow of its former self by the morning. Some pastes can shrink as much as 10-15%.

Dust with colour when the cold porcelain is just starting to firm and before it is dry.

Be aware that the colour will become darker as shrinkage happens as it will be absorbed into the paste. This being the case it is better to make the base colour pale (unless you are looking for a really dark starting point) and dust up to depth.

Use up leftover pieces of porcelain for berries, rose centres, etc. Do not add them into new porcelain otherwise you will just get lumps.

Varnishing

Steaming - for Sugar

You can achieve different degrees of shine from holding your leaf or flower over a steaming kettle. A short burst of steam seals the colour and gives a matt finish. The longer you hold over the steam the higher the shine, however be careful as the sugar will absorb the moisture and hold it too long and your leaf will drop off.

Confectioner's Varnish - for Sugar and Cold Porcelain

To achieve a very high gloss shine, eg. on Blackberries, dip your berry into full strength confectioner's varnish. Remove and spin the stem between your fingers and thumb to get rid of excess varnish. (I have a large jar which I use to do this to avoid spraying the varnish everywhere).

To achieve a softer shine eg. on acorns and hypericum berries, mix equal quantities of confectioner's varnish with iso-propyl alcohol (available from chemists) to get ½ strength varnish. You can also mix these two in ¼ and ¾ ratios (alcohol to varnish) to get varied 'shine' results, but in this project I have only used full and half strength glaze.

PME Edible Glaze - Comes in a spray can, easy to use and gives a gloss finish.

Spray Glaze - for Cold Porcelain only

Super Matt Sealing Spray from The Cromartie Group - Comes in both gloss or matt finish. Hairspray - A cheaper alternative to the Matt Spray.

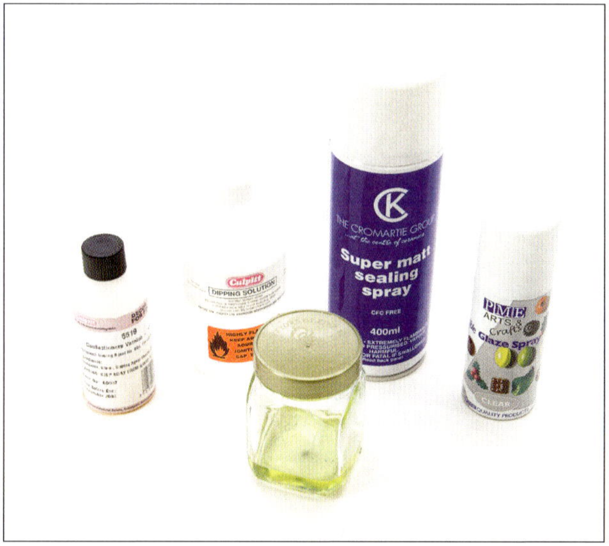

When using spray cans to varnish or for long periods of dusting with coloured powders, work in a ventilated area and wear a mask to avoid inhalation.

If using cold porcelain for a cake decoration, use a cel stick to insert spray and avoid direct contact with the cake.

And finally

If things aren't going to plan, take a break and do something else for a while. A couple of weeks in the Maldives would be nice, however a cup of tea and a walk with the dog usually works for me!

Colour Palette 1 – Used mainly for leaves

Colour Palette 2 – Used mainly for flowers, berries and older leaves

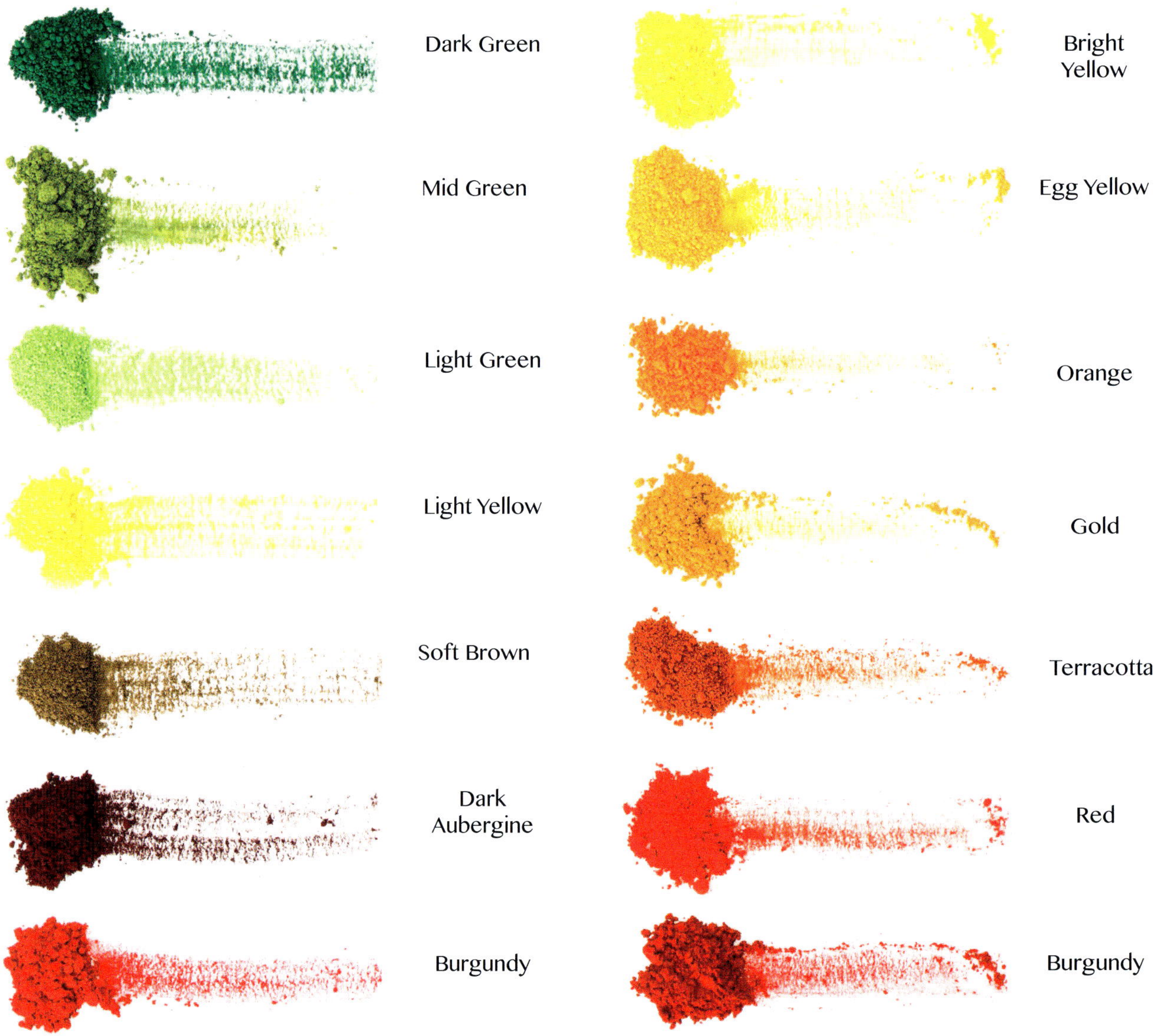

plus black and white with both palettes

Colouring

Flowers and foliage come to life when you give them colour. All colouring within this project has been done using mixes of edible colour dusting powders shown on the palettes opposite. Use these as a starting point but don't be afraid to mix other shades and experiment to get the colours you want. You will see in the photographs how the colours have been applied and there is instruction on each page of which colour palette to start with.

Liquid colour for your paste

In addition to white, you will need 4 base colours for the paste - cream, green, yellow and purple.

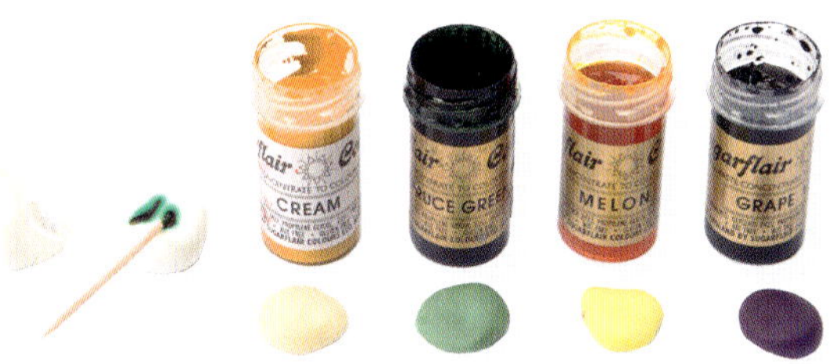

Using colour dusts

1. Put a little dust onto a kitchen paper towel, dip in brush and tap off the excess to avoid applying too much at once.

2. Always dust from the bottom upwards to give a smooth even finish. Keep a couple of brushes to use to mix colours.

3. Dust when the petals or leaves are still damp so they will absorb the colour.

4. Experiment with colours. If you put darker colours on first, it will not be easy to lift the shade by adding lighter colours on top. Start with a lighter colour and you will have more control by adding depth and shading.

5. To make a paint, mix colour dust with a little water or clear alcohol (gin/vodka). Be careful not to make it too runny. Alternatively use a commercial edible liquid paint.

6. To make your own pollen, put some fine semolina into a small clear pot with a lid. Add in some colour dust and shake well. The depth of colour is controlled by the amount of colour dust used.

7. For colour dusts and liquid paints for hand painting have a look at the fantastic range from The Sugar Mill – (see Page 76) I find that these work very well for both cold porcelain and sugar paste.

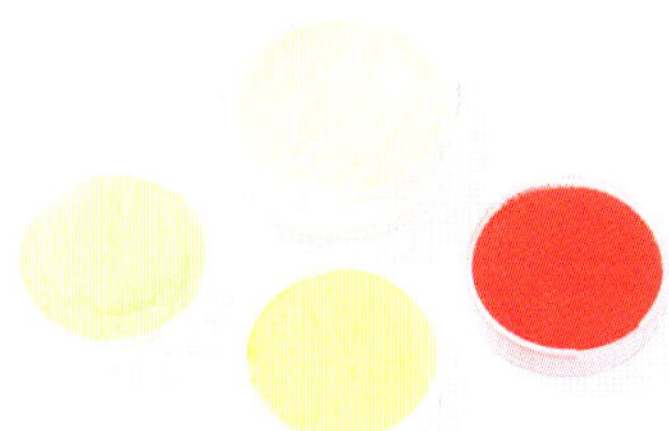

Remember that you are the Artist and you have control.

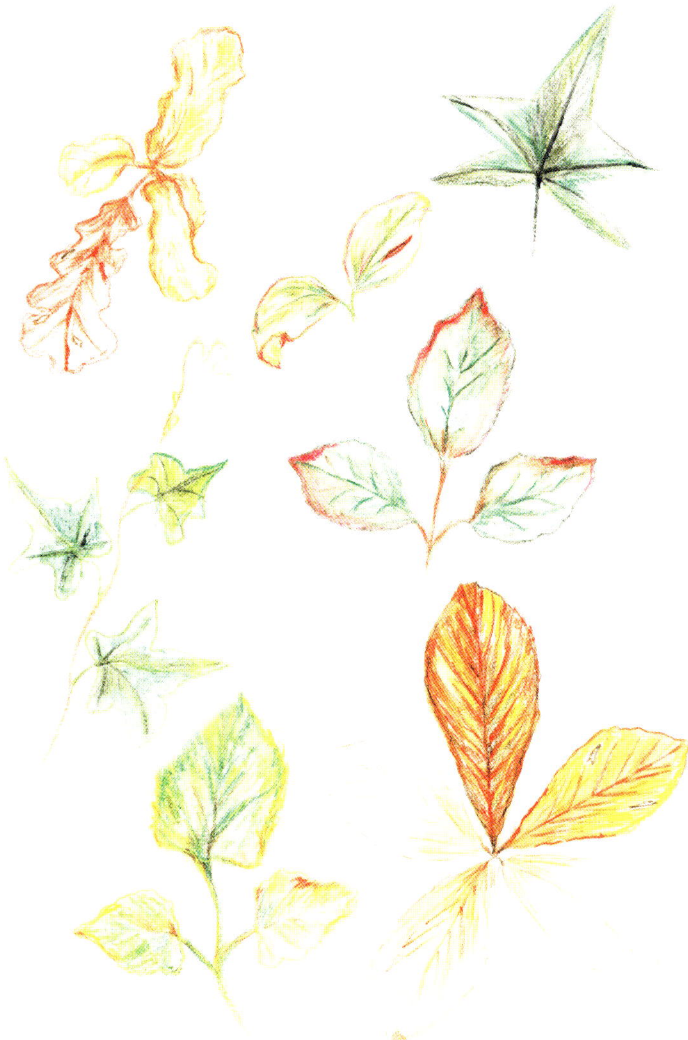

Steps to make a leaf

All the leaves within this project are made in the same way. It is only the shape and the colouring that makes the difference. To avoid repetition, I have demonstrated on the following pages how to make a leaf and achieve these results. Details of colouring suggestions, cutters and gauge of wire to use are outlined on the appropriate story page.

Double sided veiners have been used for all the leaves throughout this book. On page 17 you will find instruction on a hooked wire, a cone and a hat which are also referred to within this project. If you are having any difficulty and would like to see a short video of how these are made and also how to start taping a stem, go to www.alyson-reynolds.com and click on the appropriate link.

Equipment

Leaf cutters and veiners
Ball tool
Cel stick
Scalpel
Colouring brushes

Materials

Pale green or cream paste
24, 26 & 28g green wire
Green florist tape
Colour palette 1 & 2

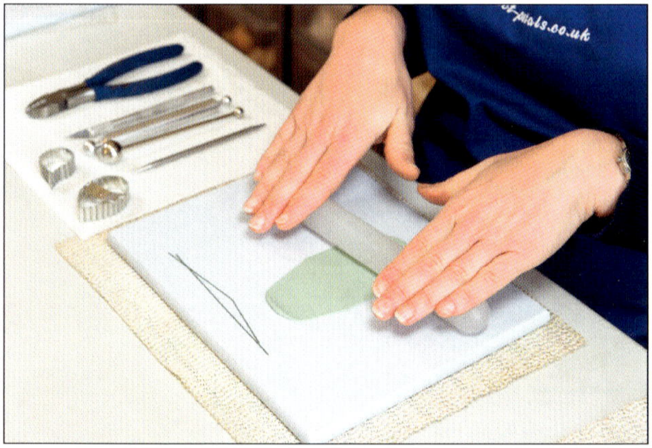

1. Cut florist wire into 4 equal lengths. Use 28g for a small leaf and up to 24g for a larger leaf. Roll out some paste leaving a slightly thicker layer at one end if you are not using a grooved board.

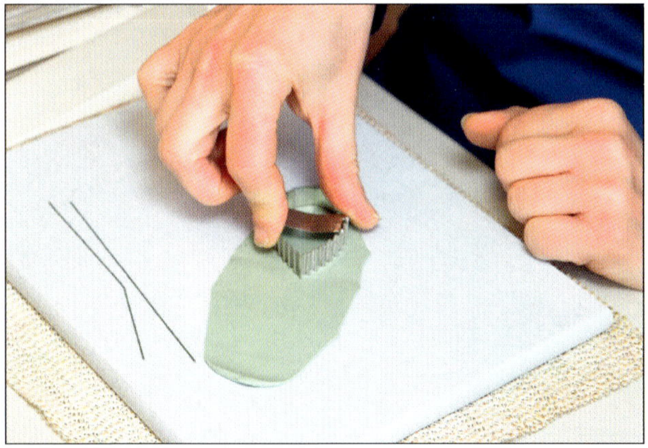

2. Cut out the shape of your leaf freehand or with a cutter.

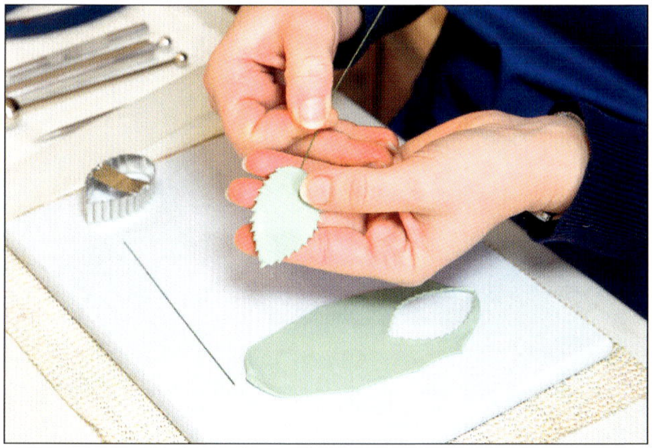

3. Insert a glued wire up from the thick end of the leaf far enough to support the weight and size (5-7mm for a small leaf and 1-2cm for larger leaves).

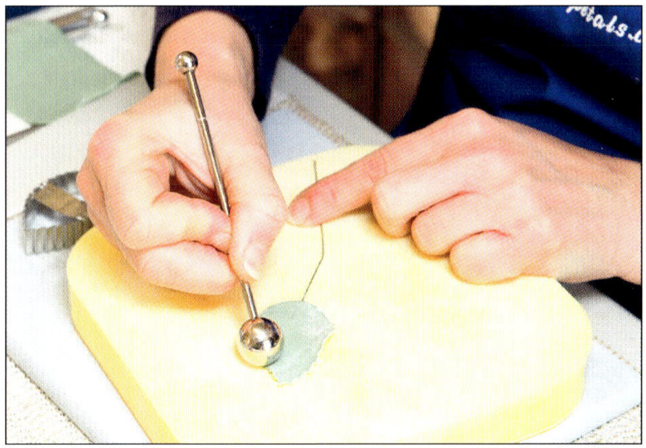

4. Place onto a cel pad and soften the edges with a ball tool. Alternatively, place onto one hand using the ball of the other hand to soften.

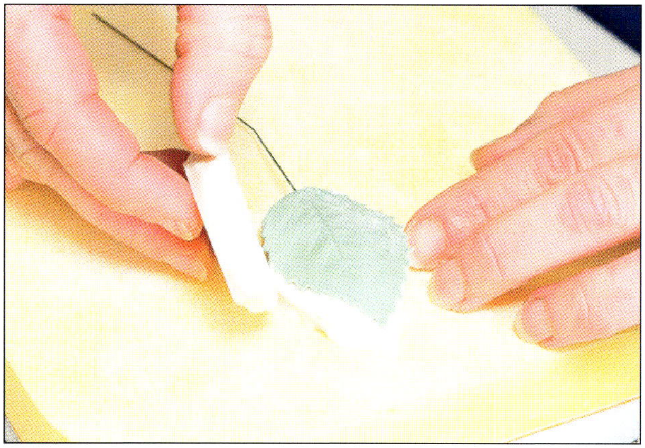

5. Lay the leaf onto the back veiner – usually the deeply grooved one – positioning the wire down the central vein. Cover with the top veiner and press gently.

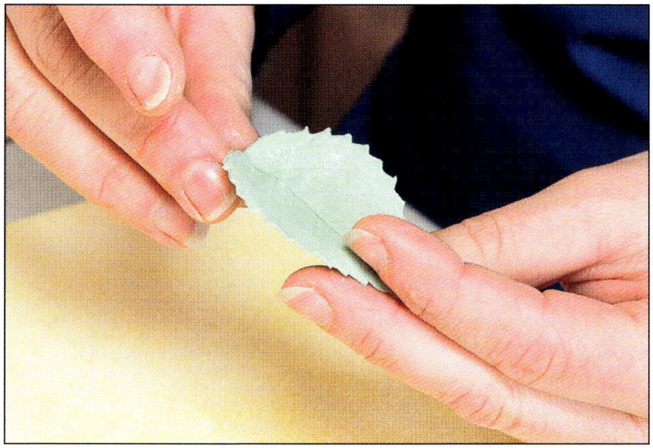

6. Use your fingers to shape and give movement to the leaf by gently twisting and bending.

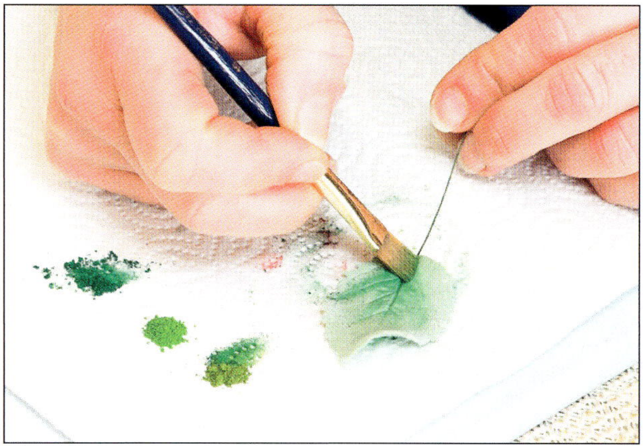

7. Dust with the appropriate colour palette, starting at the bottom of the leaf and dusting up, through the veins to highlight. Remember leaves are usually slightly lighter on the back.

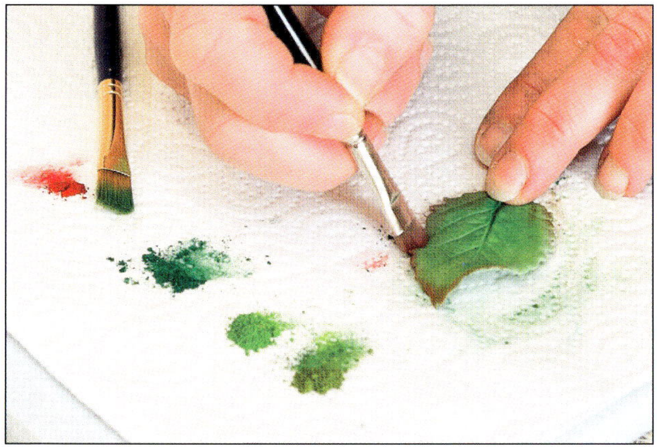

8. Add a little red or aubergine around the edges to help show movement and definition. When you have finished dusting, lie your leaf over some crumpled paper to keep the shape and allow to dry.

How to achieve different effects

To get a 'crinkled edge' on your leaf, use a cel stick to roll firmly around the edge. Highlight the 'crinkle' with another colour, either lighter or darker than the main leaf.

To create a leaf to look like it has been nibbled or split, make a small cut through the front with a scalpel. Open it up slightly and dust around the edges of the split using a mix of dark green and aubergine.

Making a small tear along the edge of the leaf at an angle can be equally as effective and using different colours to highlight the tear gives another wonderful view of nature in it's true form.

For leaves made with cream or pale paste, such as the Oak leaves, use Colour Palette 2 starting with golden colours and build with terracotta, orange, red and brown.

For leaves made in green paste use Colour Palette 1 starting with mid green and dust from the centre out to the edge, build up with darker greens along the central vein.

A hooked wire

A hooked wire helps to make a secure bond between paste and wire.

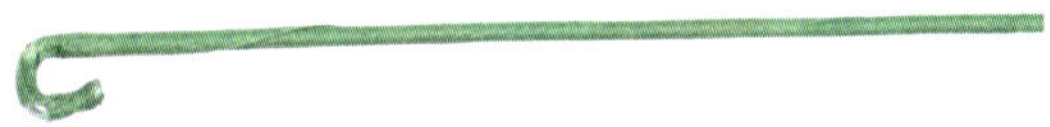

A cone

This is often used for rose centres and the beginning of a hat.

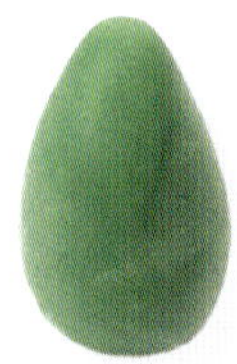

A hat

From a cone use either your fingers or a cel stick to press out the bottom into an even flat round shape. A cutter will sit over the top and leave the pointed hat in place.

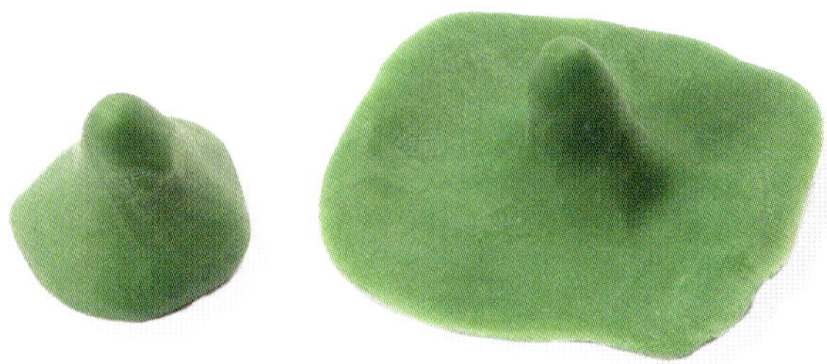

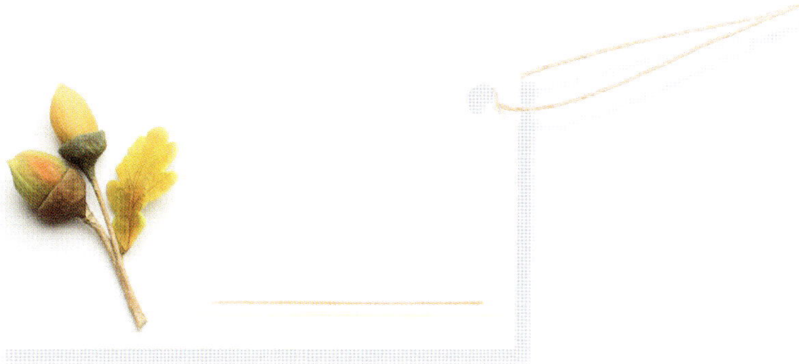

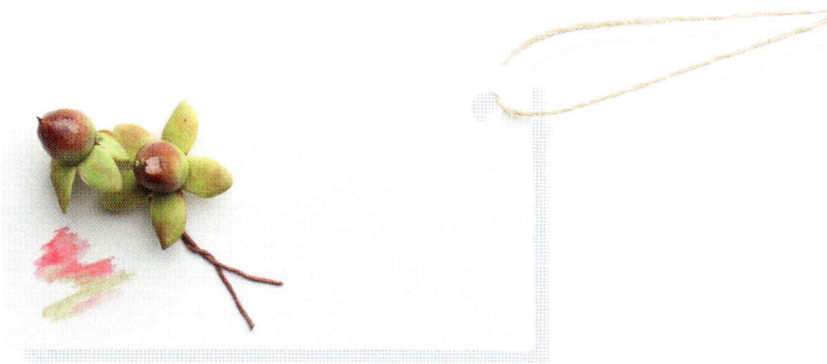

Stories

Story 1 - A Rose from your garden - or next doors

Story 2 - Rose Hips and leaves - in all shapes and sizes

Story 3 - Blackberry flowers, fruits and foliage - yummy!

Story 4 - Acorns and Oak leaves – from little acorns - who knows?

Story 5 - Stems of Honeysuckle - fragrant and romantic

Story 6 - Hypericum buds and berries - the calming effect

Story 7 - Monbretia stems - slim and elegant (in my dreams!)

Story 8 - Ivy leaves and berries – holding it all together

Story 9 - Conkers and Horse Chestnut leaves
– reminds me of my childhood

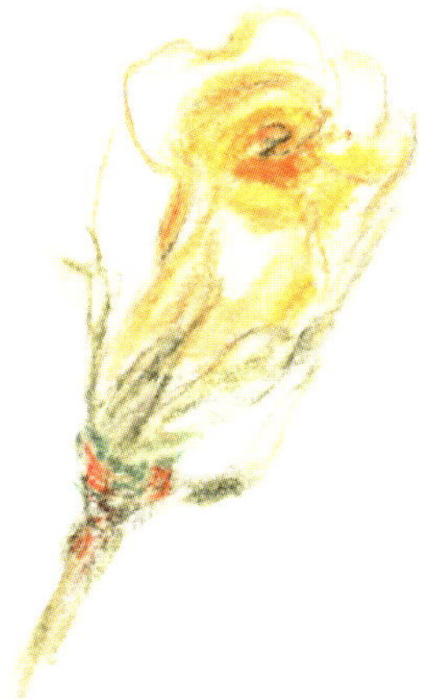

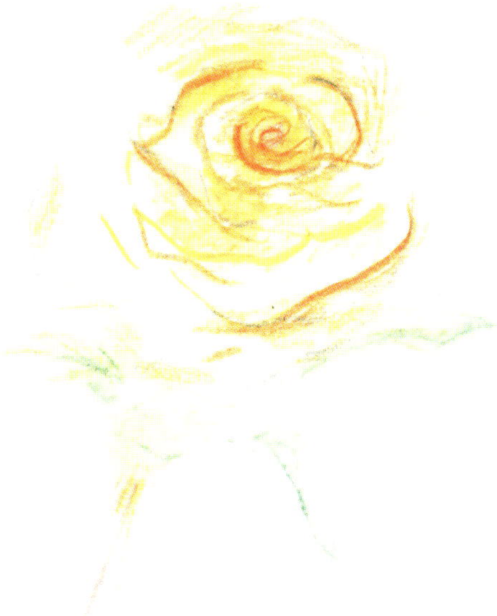

Story No. 1

A Rose from your garden - or next doors

As young girls, my sisters and I enjoyed making our own perfume by squashing petals in jam jars. Whilst staying with our Grandmother one holiday, we decided she deserved a homemade gift. We very carefully picked all the petals off her beautiful roses and proudly presented her with a salad bowl full of 'pot pouri'. She was very understanding despite the nakedness of the her garden, which thankfully was a much better reaction than the horror she expressed when she found us flogging homemade pompoms to her neighbours at the bottom of the drive!

Equipment

Ball tool, scissors or scalpel
Rose petal cutters (KB 0519 & 0052)
Rose leaf cutters (FC 570, 575 & 576)
Rose leaf veiners (SKGI)
Calyx cutters (FC 175)

Materials

Pale yellow and medium green paste
18, 20, 24 & 26g green and 24g white wire
Colour palette 1
Green florist tape

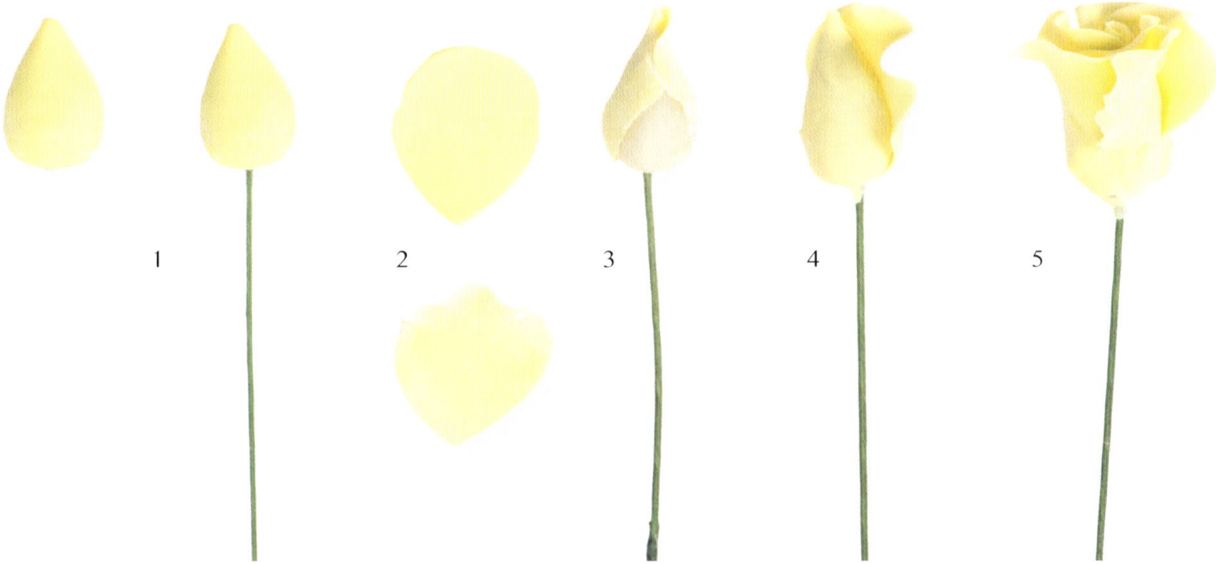

Before you start making your rose, remember to let the rose develop. Don't add in another petal because you have been told to use 7 petals. If the rose looks balanced and good at 3, 4 or 5 leave it. Keep it as a bud or start adding the next layer of larger petals.

Flowers

1. Make a centre by rolling a ball of yellow paste into a cone no larger than the smallest petal cutter you will use. Hook and glue a 18g or 20g wire (depending on size of rose) and insert into the base of the cone. Leave to dry.

2. Cut out 5-7 petals with the smallest cutter. Soften the edges and then by holding a ball tool like a pencil, half on and half off the paste, roll around the edge of the petal which will make it curl. Turn the petal over so when you place it against the cone the part curling outwards will be at the top curling slightly backwards.

3. Glue the cone and place the first petal slightly raised against the cone, folding it around tightly, and secure.

4. Glue over the join of the 1st petal and place the second petal to the right of the join, wrapping to the left and leave slightly open in order to insert the next petal. Continue with the other petals creating a spiral effect. Keep the petals with their backs curling outwards.

5. Repeat the process with the next size of petal cutter, allowing the rose to open up as you continue. Use as many petals as you need to keep an even shape. As you build the rose with the different size cutters, place the petals slightly lower than the previous layer to show the rose opening out.

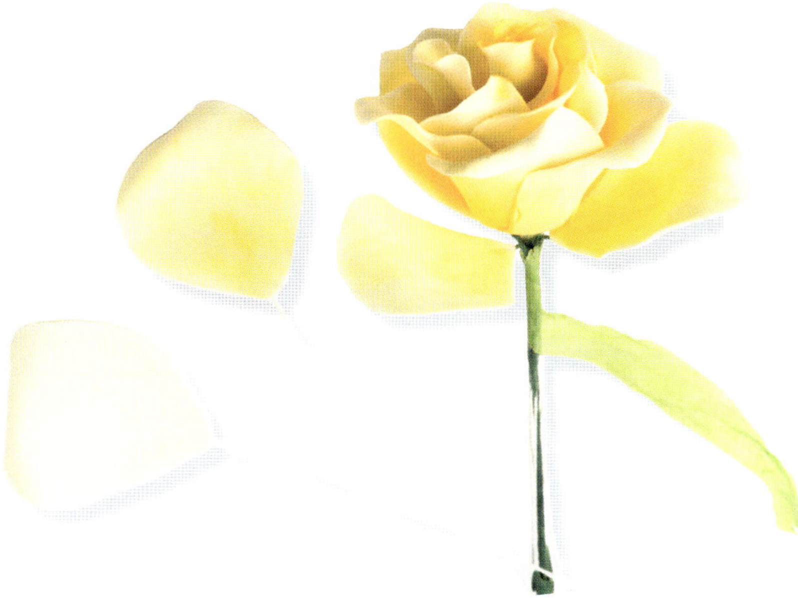

6

Wired Petals

6. For a large rose, you may wish to add wired petals. From pale yellow paste, cut out 6 petals and insert a 24g white wire. Lay the petal on your hand and soften the edges. Gently cup the petal with your thumb or ball tool. Turn the petal over and curl the top back with your fingers or a ball tool. The cup of the petal will fit neatly round the base as shown. Leave to dry in a position to keep the shape - an apple tray is quite useful. Cut out as many petals as you need, 5 or 6 should do it, but remember, use however many you need.

Colouring

7. Colour the rose petals before adding the calyx. Dust each petal from the bottom up, darker in the middle and shading lighter on either side. The centre of the rose is stronger in colour than the outer petals so lighten the colour palette as you dust outwards. Dust with deep yellows to pale and lightly dust some red or orange on the outside edges of the petals.

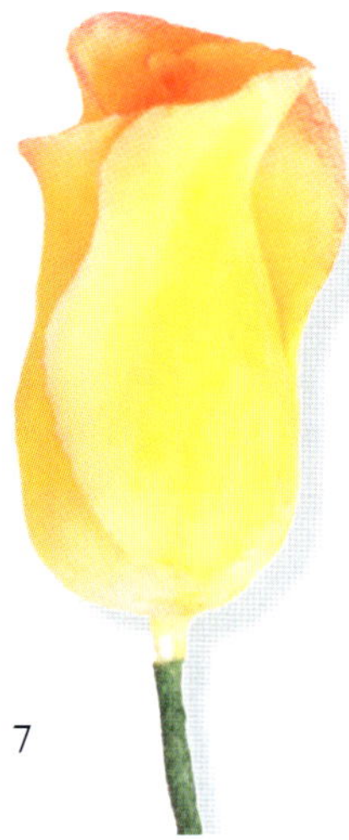

7

Calyx

8. Roll out some green paste, cut out a calyx to suit your rose.

9. With a scalpel or scissors, cut slits into the edge of some of the sepals and dust the main calyx with greens. Brush aubergine/red along the edges to catch the cuts in the sepals.

10. Roll a small cone of green paste for the hip.

11. Insert the rose down through the centre of the calyx adding a little glue to the base of the calyx to stick. Finally, insert the stem of the rose down through the hip, push into position shape into a hip and pinch off any extra paste. Dust to match the calyx.

8

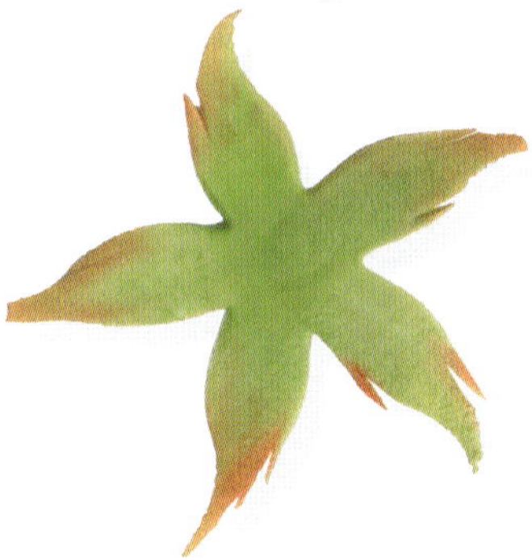

9

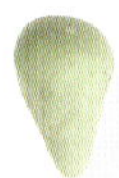

10

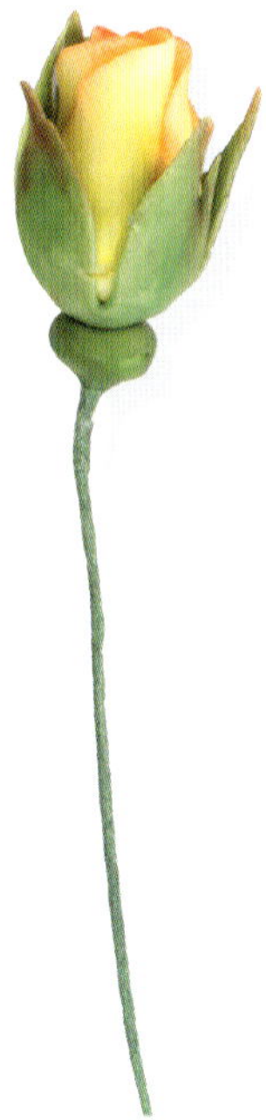

11

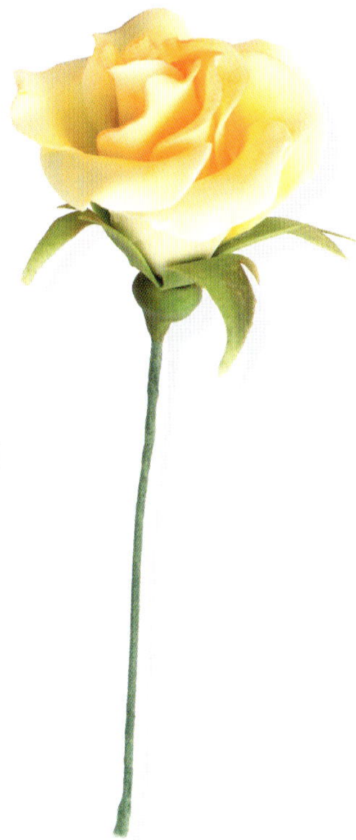

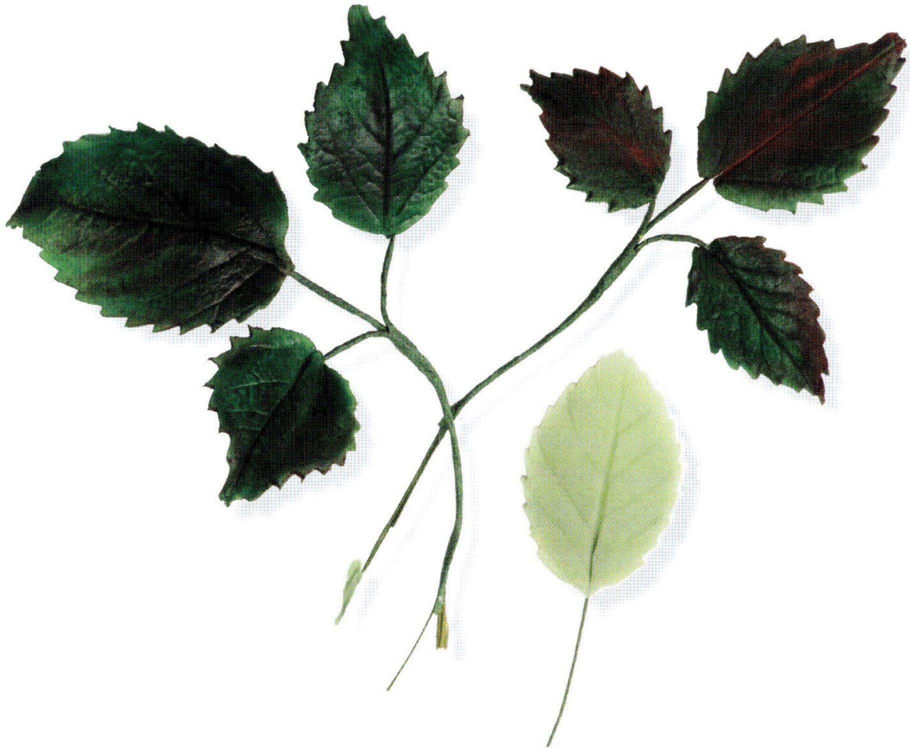

Leaves

12. Refer to the instructions on Pages 14-17 .

13. Cut 24 & 26g wires into 4. From mid green paste make 3 large and 6 medium leaves, vein and colour with shades of green and edge with aubergine and red using colour palette no. 1. Tape 25mm down stem with green florist tape.

14. Tape leaves into groups of 3 using 1 large and 2 medium either side.

Assembly

15. Tape the leaves and the roses together using beige or green florist tape. If you use beige tape, dust with a little green and red to give depth and variety.

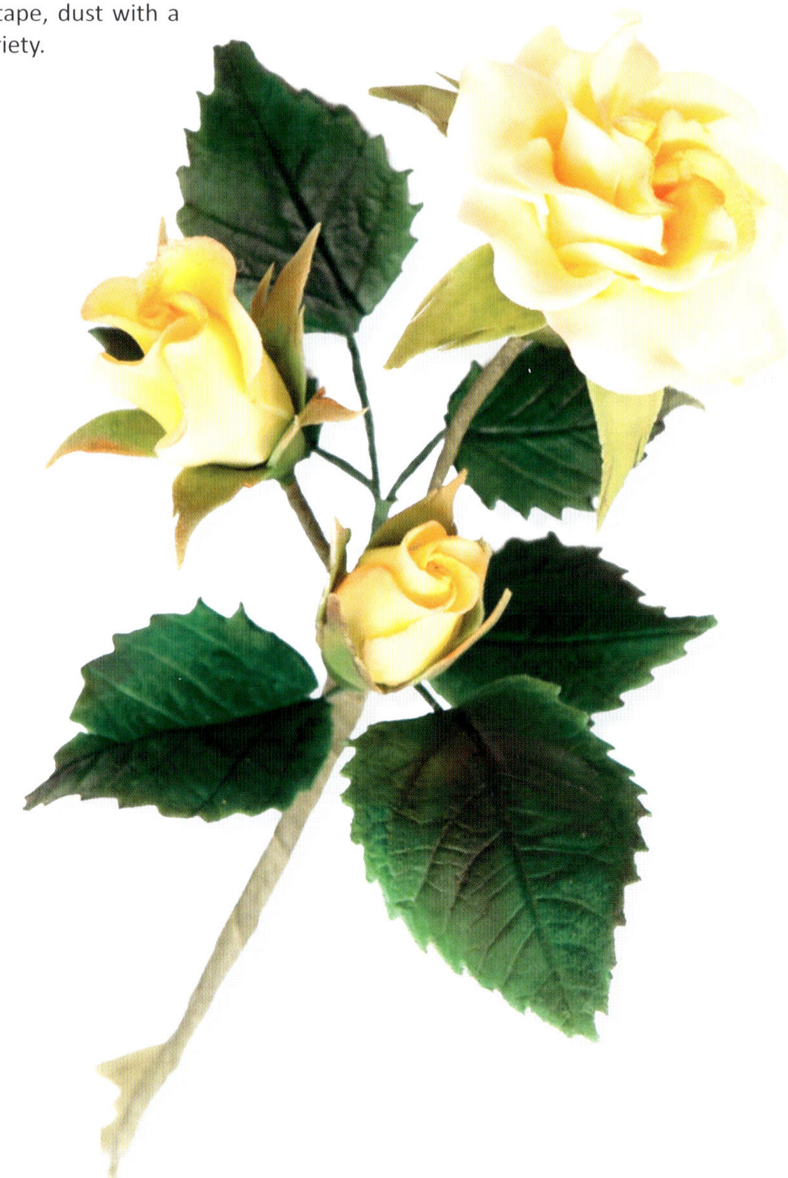

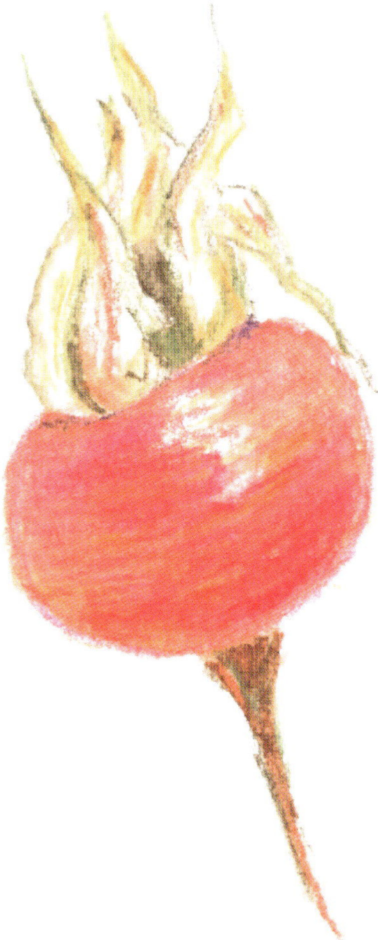

Story No. 2

Rose Hips and leaves - in all shapes and sizes

Rosehips guarantee a display to rival the flowers they have replaced. Varying in shape and size their colours range from green to yellow, orange and red offering an element of fun to be included within many arrangements. Well known for their medicinal benefits they are also delicious served at the table or instilled with a touch of gin or vodka to warm the cockles of your heart.

Equipment

Ball tool, scissors or scalpel
5 petal calyx cutter (FC - several sizes)
Rose leaf cutters (FC 570, 575 & 576)
Rose leaf veiners (SKGI)

Materials

Cream and mid-green paste
Dark red or brown cotton thread
Nile green florist tape, matches
20, 22, 26 and 28g wires
Colours palette 1 & 2
Confectioners varnish

1 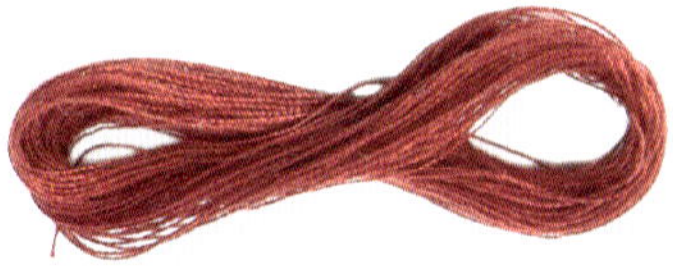

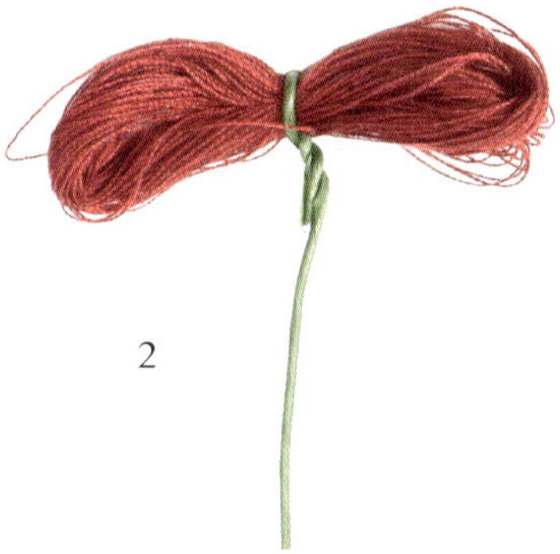
2

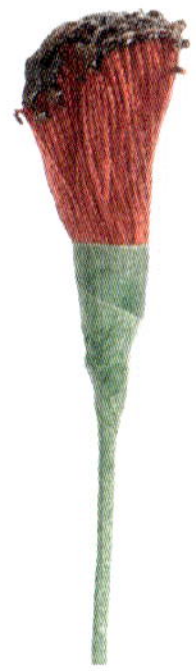
3

Centre tuft

1. Wrap thread around two fingers approx. 50 times. Twist into a figure of eight.

2. Bend a piece of 20g wire around the middle and twist wire to secure. Bend threads upwards and tape. Cut threads with scissors to make a tuft.

3. Carefully burn the top of the thread with a match which will melt the thread and form the dead centre of the hip. Weight of wire will depend on size of rose hip. Bigger the hip, the stronger the wire.

4 

5 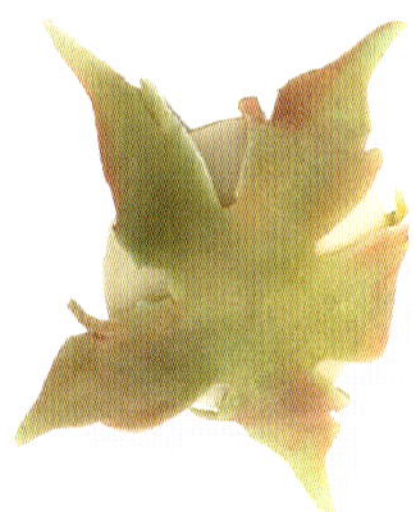

6 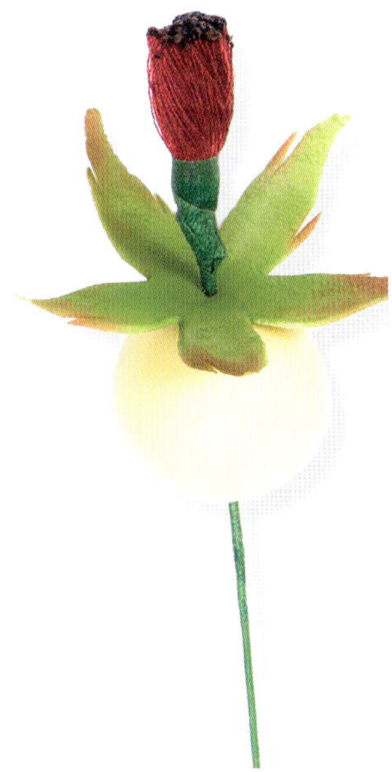

Making the hip

4. Roll a piece of cream porcelain into a ball.

5. From green porcelain, cut out a calyx and snip edges with scissors, dust with greens and browns and lay over the top of the ball.

6. Insert the rose hip centre through the calyx and ball from the top and ease the calyx up into position.

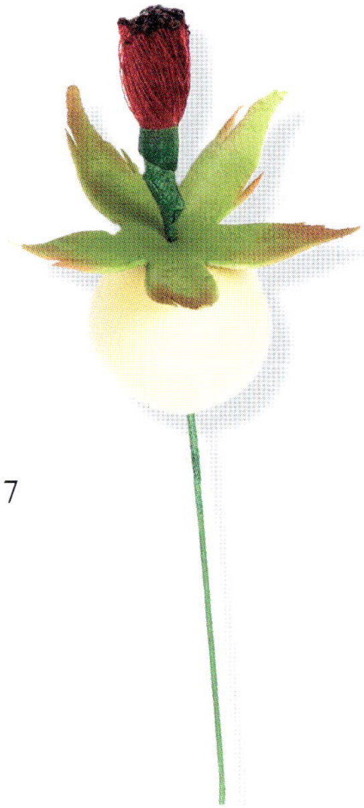

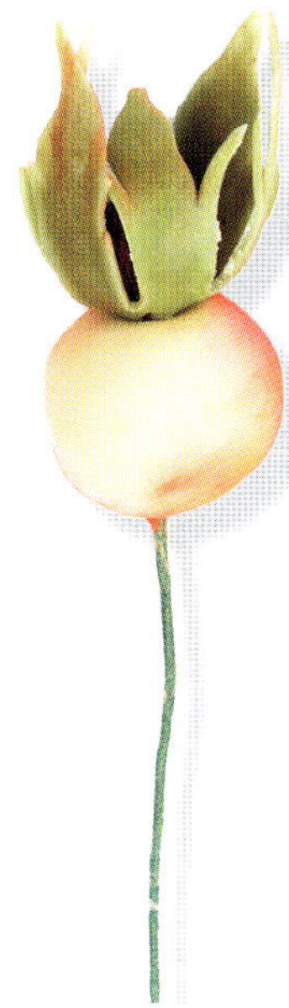

7

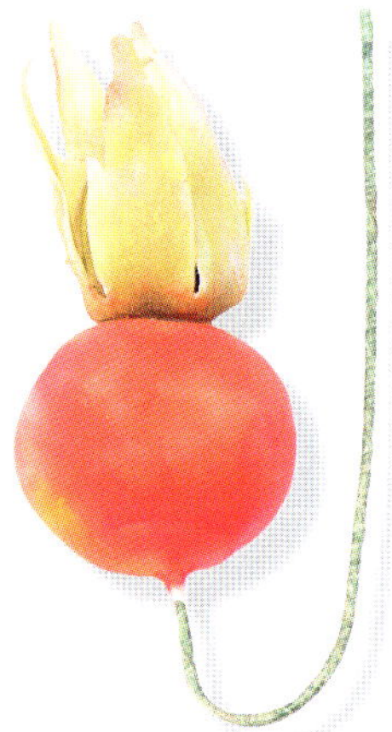

8

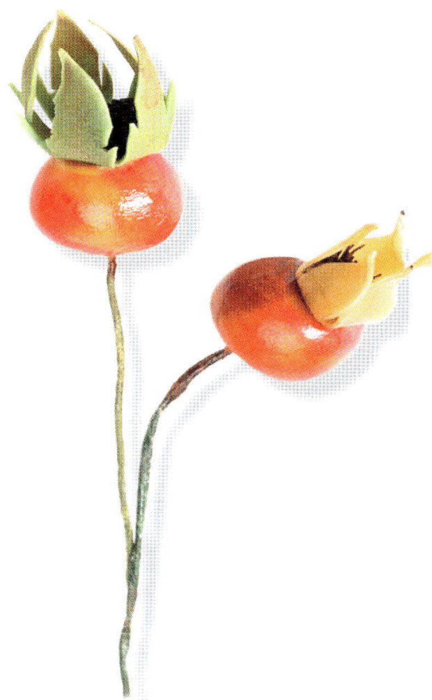

Colouring

7. Dust the ball of the hip with a mixture of reds, yellows and oranges. Hang the hip upside down to dry and this will help to set the correct shape.

Glazing

8. Either bend the wire and dip ONLY the ball of the hip into full glaze, carefully avoiding the calyx or, if you prefer, using an old dusting brush, paint the ball of the hip with the glaze and leave to dry.

Leaves

9. Refer to the instructions on Pages 14-17.

10. Cut 24 & 26g wires into 4. From mid green paste, cut out 3 large and 6 medium leaves, vein and colour them with softer shades of green to enhance their age. Edge the leaves with aubergine and red using colour palette 1. Tape down the stem with green florist tape.

11. Tape leaves into groups of 3 using 1 large and 2 medium either side.

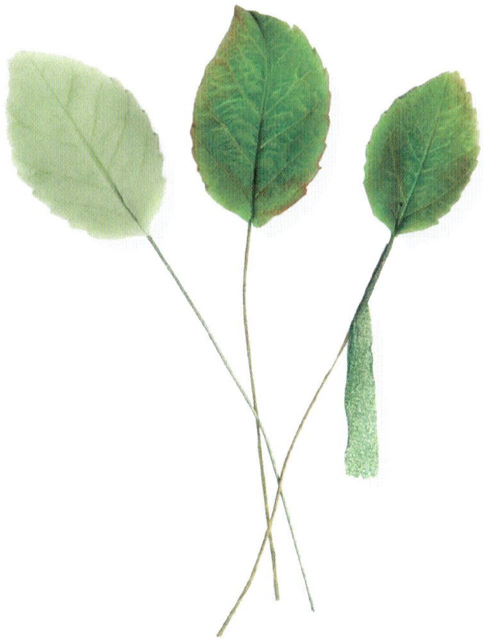

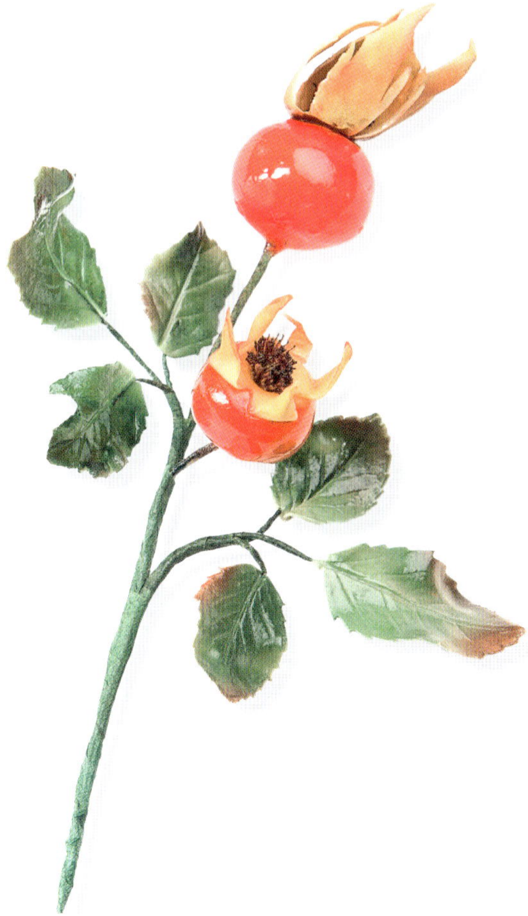

Assembly

12. Tape the rosehips and leaves together with ½ width green florist tape.

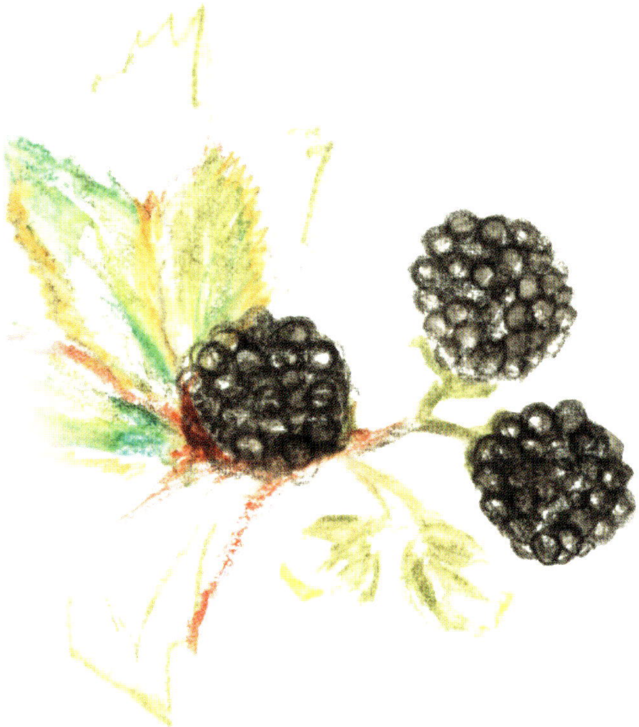

Story No. 3

Blackberry flowers, fruits and foliage - yummy!

The hedgerows are filled with another wonderful offering from Mother Nature to tickle the taste buds and please the eye. Following a wholesome walk picking berries on a crisp morning and returning home to the smell of the Sunday roast sizzling in the oven, the anticipation of the blackberry and apple crumble to follow is almost too much to bare.

Equipment

Ball tool, cel stick, veining tool
5 petal blossom cutter (KB 07 & 02)
Rose leaf cutters (FMM RL2 & RL3)
Calyx cutters (FC 165 set of 3)
Blackberry leaf veiners (SKGI)

Materials

24, 26 & 28g wires
White, purple and green paste
Yellow and white cotton
Yellow pollen
Colour palette 1
Confectioners varnish or PME edible glaze
Nile green florist tape

Buds

1. From white paste roll a pea size ball and insert a 28g green wire. Put a little glue on the top of the ball and dip into yellow pollen.

2. Cut out a small calyx.

3. Insert the wired ball through the centre and secure tightly around the bud, letting the pollen peep out from the top. Dust the calyx with shades of green.

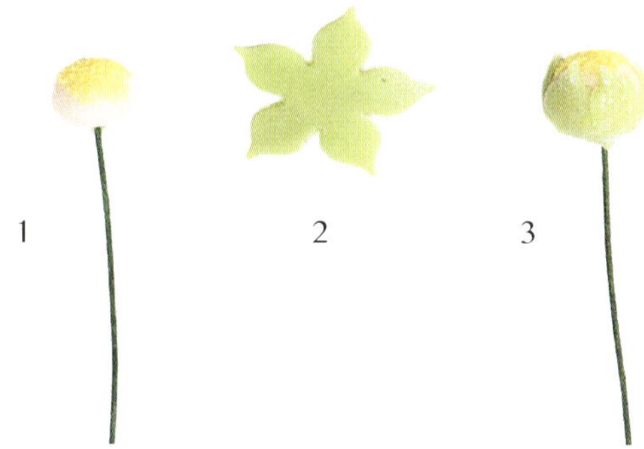

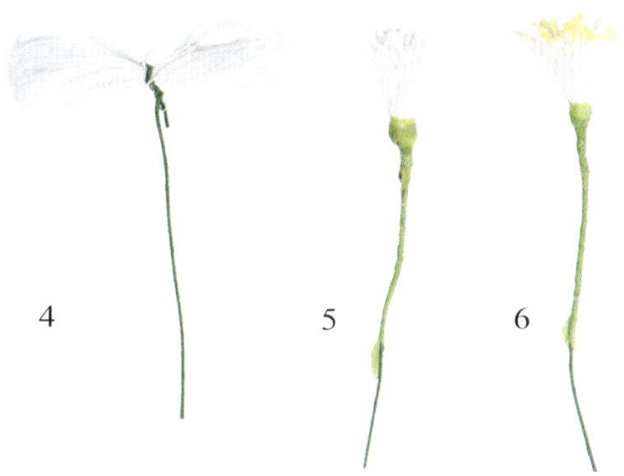

Stamens

4. Wrap white cotton around two fingers approx. 30 times. Twist into a figure of eight and bend a piece of 28g wire around the middle and twist the wire to secure.

5. Bend threads upwards and tape with ½ width nile green florist tape.

6. Brush a little glue over the top of the threads and dip into yellow pollen mix.

Flowers

7. Cut out a 5 petal blossom, soften and spread the individual petals using a ball tool. For a different effect, frill the edges with a cell stick.

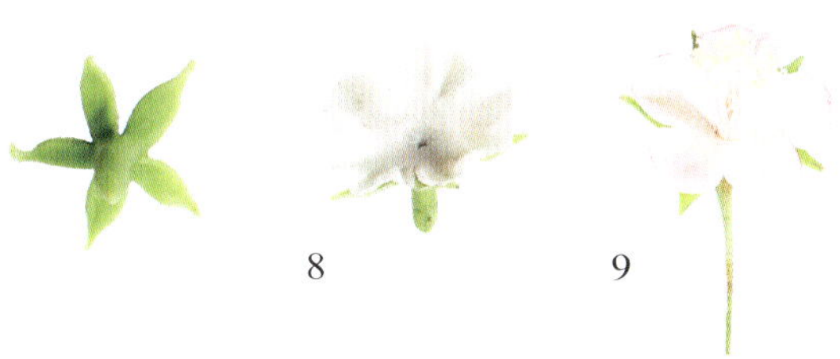

8. From green paste make a hat and cut out a calyx. Dab a little glue onto the centre of the calyx and place the petal over the top.

9. Insert the wired threads down through the centre of the flower. Tape stem with ¼ width nile green tape. Dust the petal with white adding a little pink around the edge.

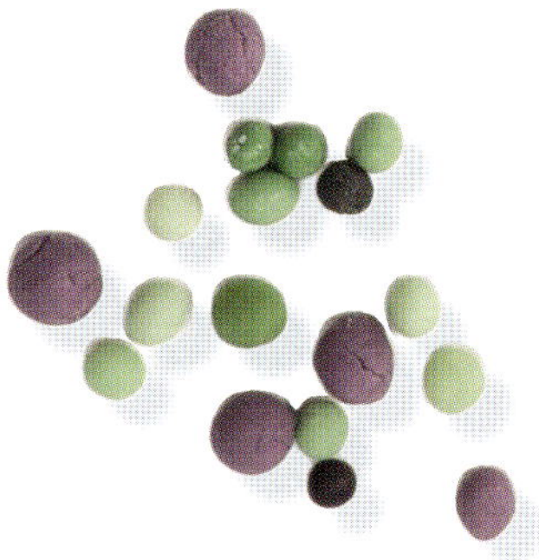

Blackberries

10. From black, green or purple paste, roll lots of little balls of similar sizes to be the pips. (I usually save this to the evenings as an excuse to sit down with a glass of wine in front of the telly with no guilt at all.) Leave the pips to dry.

11. Insert a 24g wire into a ball of green or purple/black paste about the diameter of a 5p coin (18mm).

12. Cover the ball with glue and with tweezers stick the pips individually onto it. The size of the pips you have made will dictate the size of the blackberry. So if you want really juicy looking ones make larger pips. You can mix the colours of the pips to give variation on the berry. Leave to dry.

13. Paint the blackberry by mixing black, burgundy and green coloured dusts with water/alcohol to show different stages of ripening. Dip into full glaze to give a really glossy shine. When dry, add a small calyx to the bottom and dust with green.

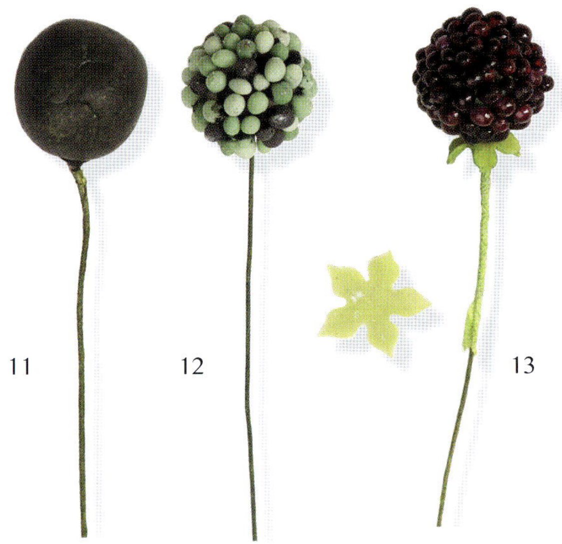

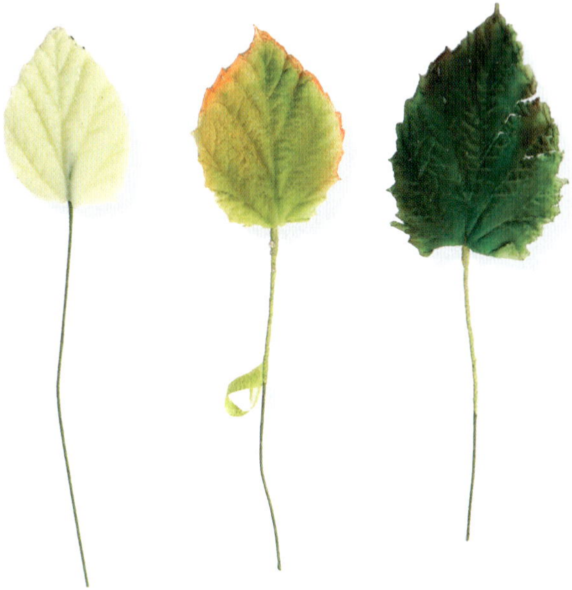

Leaves

14. Refer to the instructions on Pages 14-17.

15. Cut 26g wires into 4. Using the rose leaf cutter and blackberry veiner make leaves of two sizes on 26g wire. Cut across the bottom of the leaf before inserting the wire to give a more triangular shape. Dust with colours of greens, gold and brown to suit the season. Varnish to a matt finish. Tape into sets of 3.

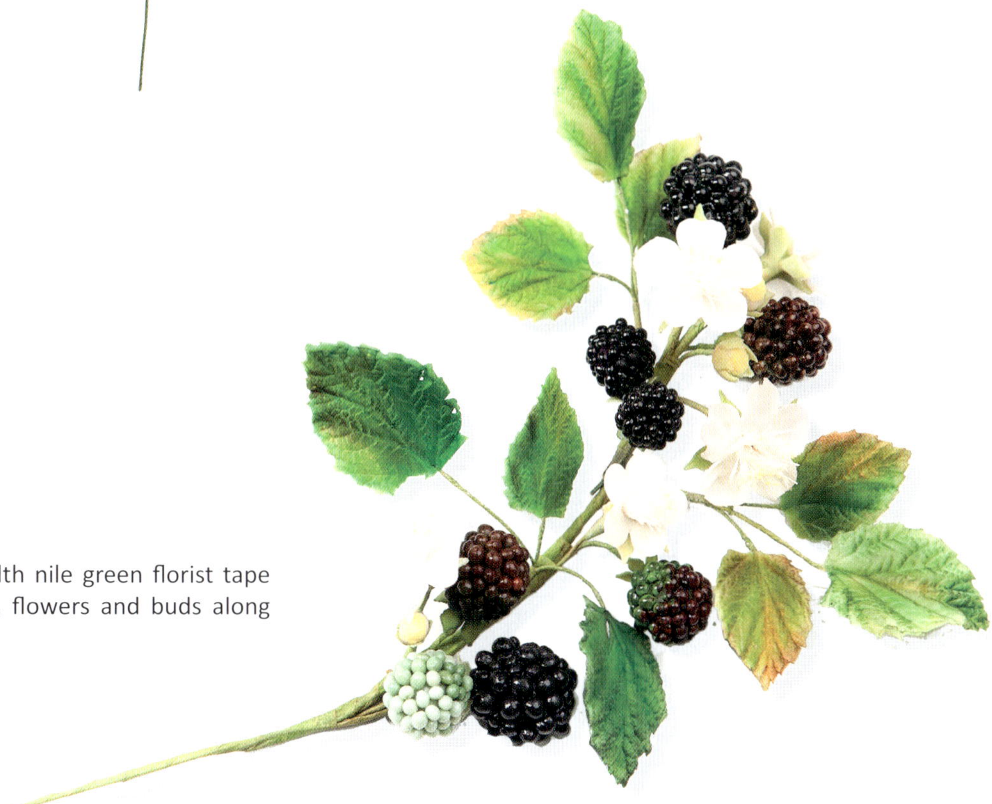

Assembly

16. Tape all stems with ¼ width nile green florist tape interspersing groups of berries, flowers and buds along the stem.

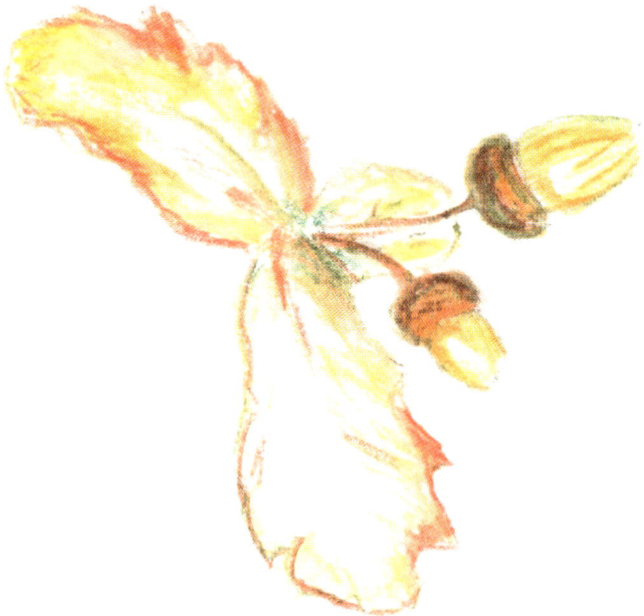

Story No. 4

Acorns and Oak leaves – from little acorns - who knows?

On moving to Scotland in 1995, the previous owners of our new home had planted an acorn in the garden which had just sprouted and was then 6 inches off the ground. Now this little acorn has turned into a beautiful Oak tree and is reaching 30 feet high. Nowhere near maturity, but it is another jaw dropping aspect of nature that demonstrates that you don't have to be big to start with, just work with what you have and the rest will follow.

Equipment

Ball tool, cel stick or veining tool
Oak leaf cutters (FMM Oak 1,2 & 3) and (FC 450, 455)
Oak leaf veiner (SKGI)

Materials

Pale cream and pale green paste
26 & 28g wires
Beige florist tape ¼ and ½ width
Colour palette 1 and 2
Gloss spray varnish

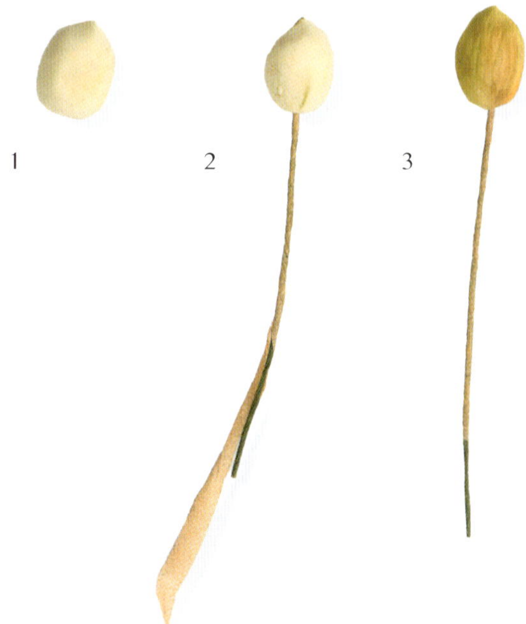

Acorns

1. Roll a ball of cream paste into an oval. Pinch the tip of one end to make a little spike.

2. Insert a hooked 26g wire and vein by drawing lines from the top to the bottom with either a cel stick or a veining tool.

3. Dust the acorn with shades of yellow, green and brown to achieve the desired colour. Young nuts are paler with yellows and greens whilst the older nuts are brown. Tape with ¼ width beige florist tape.

Cups

4. To make a cup take a small cone of green paste and hollow it out with your ball tool by gently pressing and twisting the tool.

5. When you have a nice cup shape, put a little glue in the cup and insert one of the acorns down through the centre. Gently press the cup around the acorn to secure. Be careful not to lose the rim of the cup into the acorn. With a cel stick prick the outside of the cup to make it look pitted. Dust the cup with browns and greens.

6. To make a cup on its own, make the cup as above and then hook a 28g wire and insert through the top down into the bottom until it is hidden. Use a cel stick to cover most of the hole made by the wire, leaving a mark to show where the acorn was attached. Use the cel stick to pit the outside of the cup. Tape with ¼ width beige florist tape and dust with browns and a touch of green.

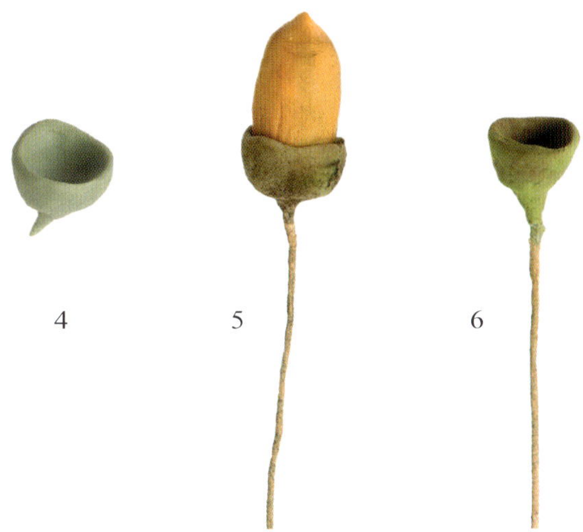

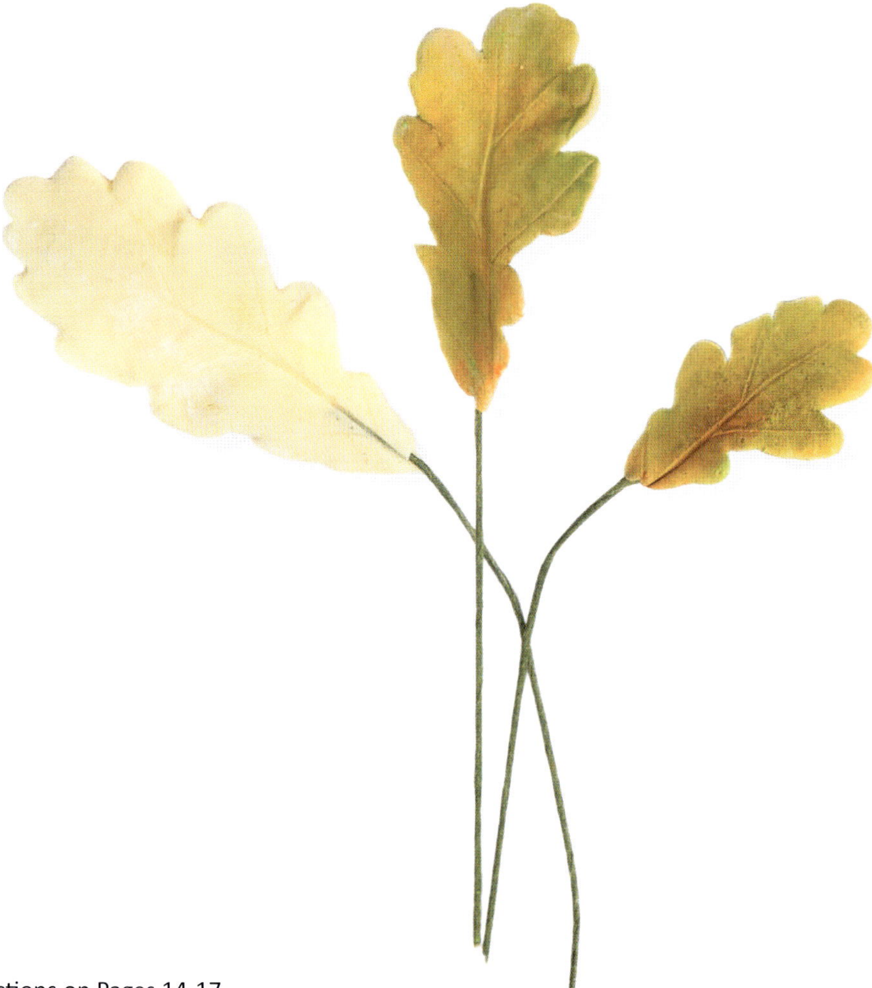

Leaves

7. Refer to the instructions on Pages 14-17.

8. From cream paste, cut out leaves. Use 26g and 28g wire cut into 5. Make a range of sizes, vein and colour with yellow, orange and a touch of green. Tape down the stem with ¼ width beige florist tape. Varnish to a matt finish.

Assembly

9. Using ½ width beige florist tape, tape a group of acorns and cups tightly together at the base. Tape the leaves either individually onto the main stem or together in small groups behind the acorns.

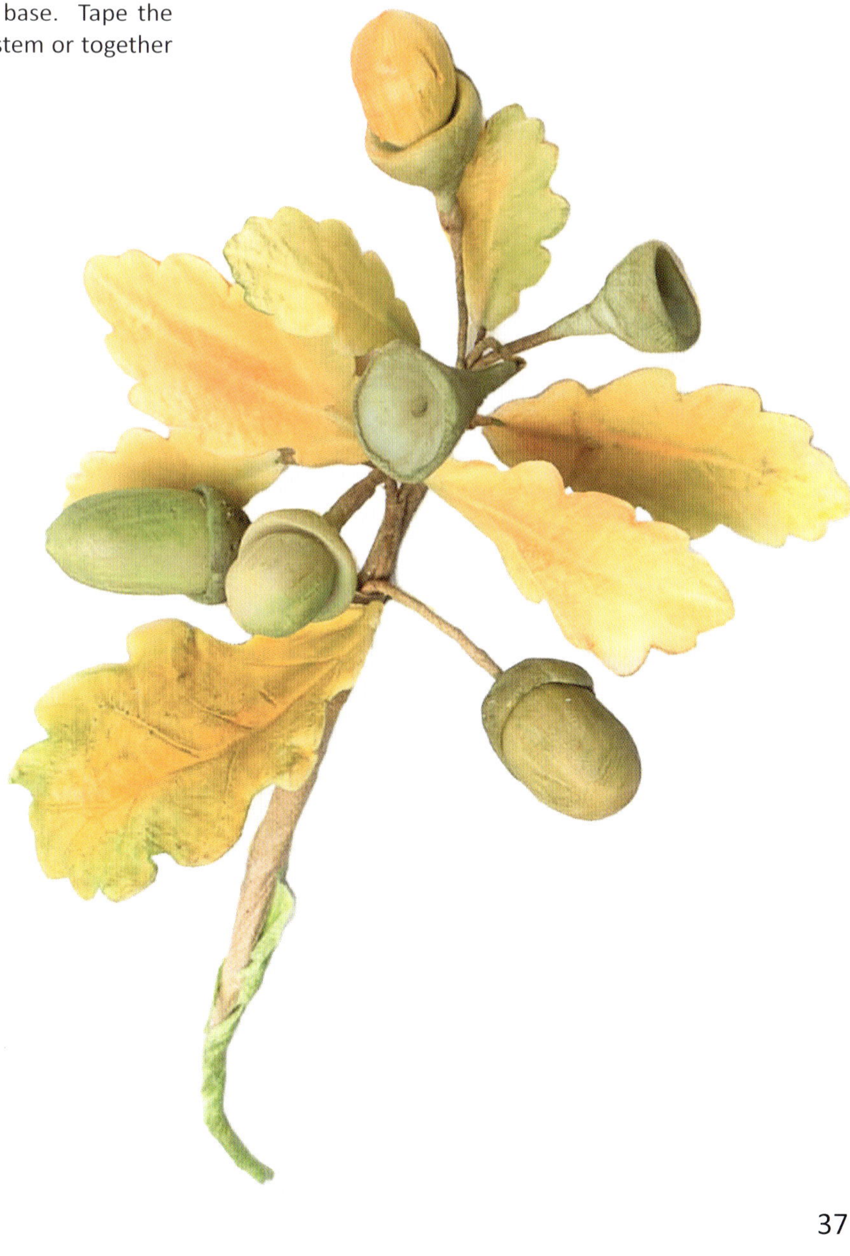

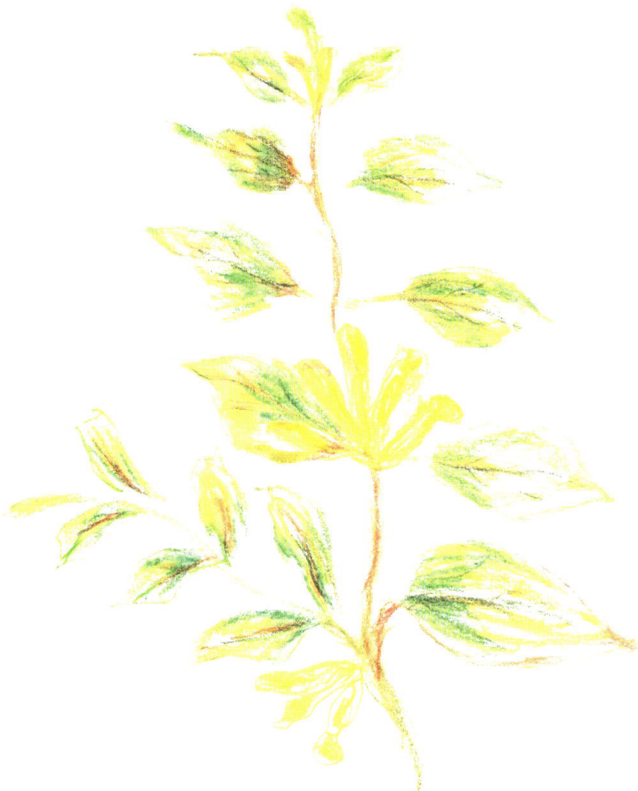

Story No. 5

Stems of Honeysuckle - fragrant and romantic

November 2011 and the honeysuckle in my garden is as confused as I am by the warm Autumn. It has new buds, blossom and remnant berries from flowering earlier in the Summer. A truly hardy plant, which not only offers an abundance of flowers, colour and a sweet fragrance but it is also a climbing plant. This is fortunate for me, as it is currently covering the car port hiding my sons' 'long term' car project. Bearing in mind it will be 2 years before the eldest can drive, the car may well disappear. (I've heard that its worth £150 at the scrap yard - shhh!)

Equipment

Cel stick
No cutters for the flowers – just your hands.
Metal leaf cutter (FC leaf set 362)
Honeysuckle leaf veiners (SKGI)

Materials

Pale yellow/Cream and green paste
26, 28 & 30g green wire and 28g white wire
Dark brown, green, red and white florist tape.
Pale cream or white embroidery or cotton thread
Stamens seedhead small white
Colour palette 2

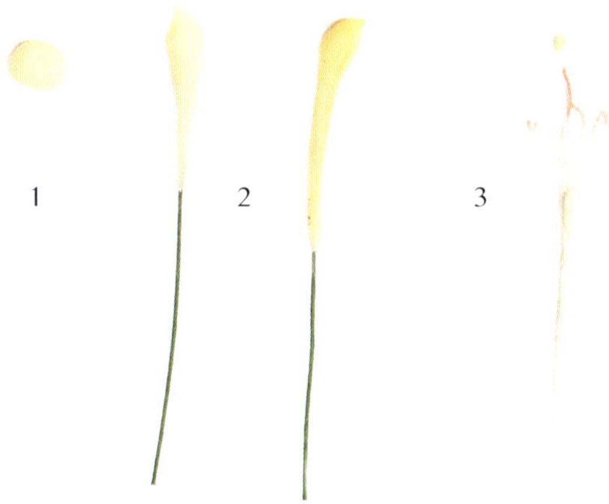

Buds

1. Roll a pea size ball of pale yellow/cream paste and insert 28g wire.

2. Tease the paste between thumb and forefinger 2-3cm down the wire leaving the majority of the paste at the top. Pinch the tip and bend the wire slightly to curve the bud. Dust with pale orange/peach and yellow.

Stamen

3. Take one small stamen, dip into glue and then into pale green pollen. Cut a 2cm length of separated embroidery thread or 6 pieces of cotton thread and dab the end with terracotta dust. Tape the thread together with the stamen onto white 28g wire with ¼ width white tape. Make sure the stamen is higher than the thread.

Flowers

4. From pale yellow/cream paste, roll a slim cone 15mm in length.

5. Make a cut with a scalpel in the fat end one third from the top.

6. Split the two open and use your fingers to gently flatten the larger piece into the shape of the main petal.

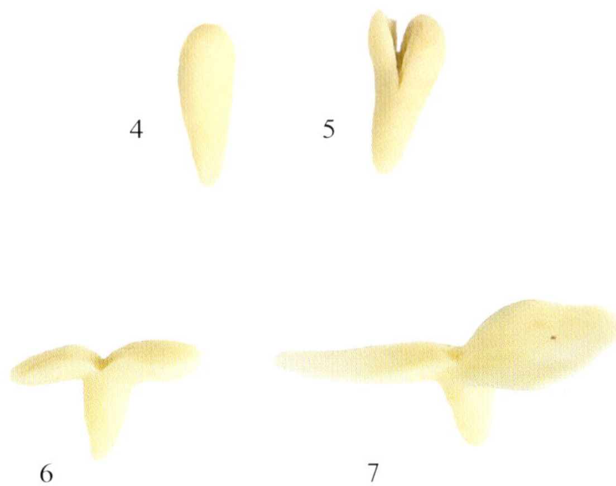

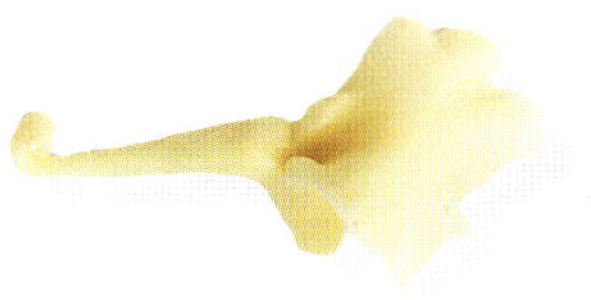

8

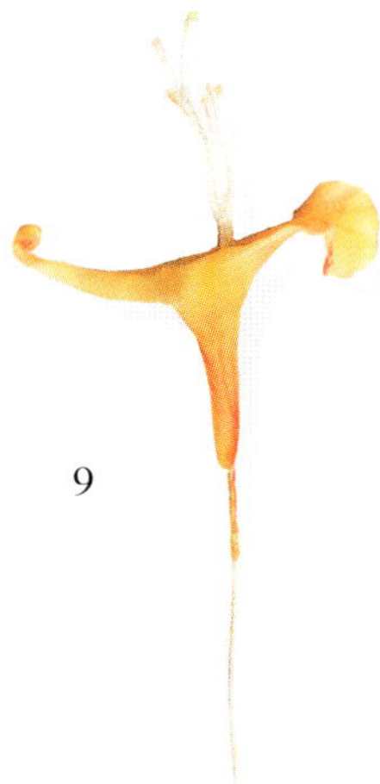

9

7. Use a cel stick and roll the thinner piece into the tail.

8. Frill the main petal with a cel stick and curl it backwards at the top. Make a small hollow for the stamen in the centre of the cone and use your cell stick to lightly vein. Shape the tail by curling up the end towards the opening of the flower.

9. Insert the stamen down through the centre and secure around the wire. Dust with peach and yellow on the main flower and edge with a little red especially at the base, the curl of the flower and at the end of the tail. Tape stem 2cm with ¼ width nile green florist tape.

Berries

10. To obtain a waxy and opaque look for these berries, do not add white acrylic/oil to the porcelain paste before use. With white paste roll 24-30 small balls in various sizes and insert a 30g green wire through the centre of each ball so it just peeps out of the top. When dry, paint with shades of red petal dusts mixed with water/alcohol. Blot in places to vary the shading. Spray with gloss varnish or dip into ¼ strength glaze.

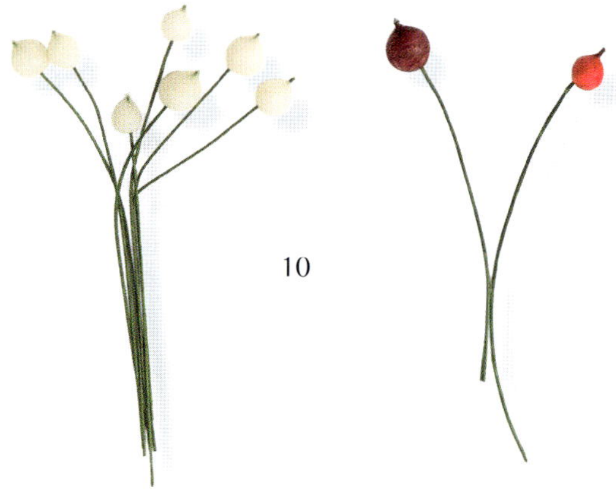

10

11. Wrap full width brown tape around the top of a 24g wire, looping it several times and secure.

12. Chop the top end with scissors.

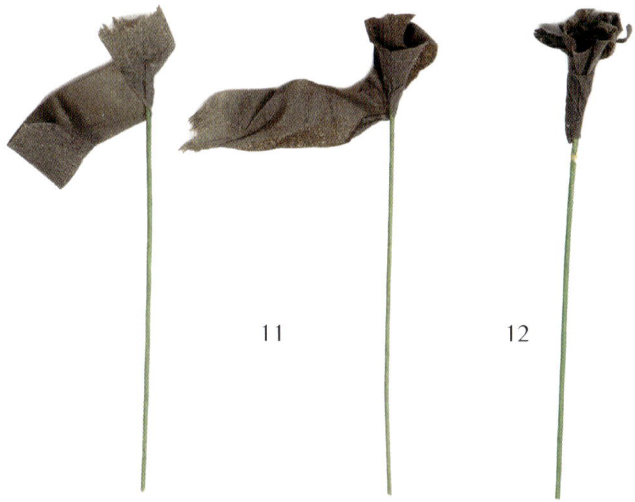

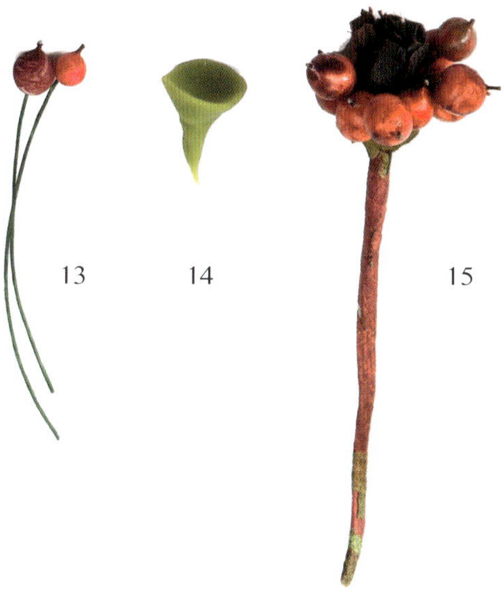

13. Place the berries around the centre and tape in groups of 2 or 3 to the stem.

14. Hollow out a small cone of green paste around a ball tool.

15. Insert the stem of berries through the top and secure. Nip little marks in the green paste. Tape the stem with ½ width red florist tape.

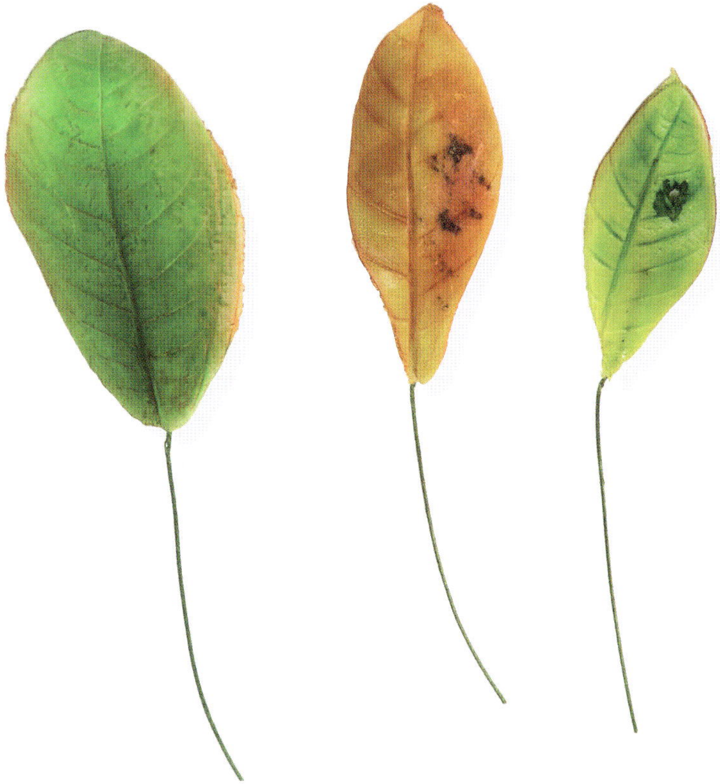

Leaves

16. Refer to the instructions on Pages 14-17.

17. Use 26 & 28g wire cut into 5. Make 6 small, 6 medium and 6 large leaves using the metal leaf cutter and honeysuckle veiner. Insert the 28g wire into the pointed end. Use your colour palette to create different stages of leaf development. Mid and spring green with a bit of yellow for the fresh new growth tailing off to yellow, gold and red for the older ones.

Assembly

18. Tape the leaves with nile green tape in pairs onto a 24g wire, adding buds in groups of 2, 3 and 5 on the way down including full flowers within the larger groups towards the lower end of the stem.

19. The red berries stand at the top of their own stems with leaves following below in pairs.

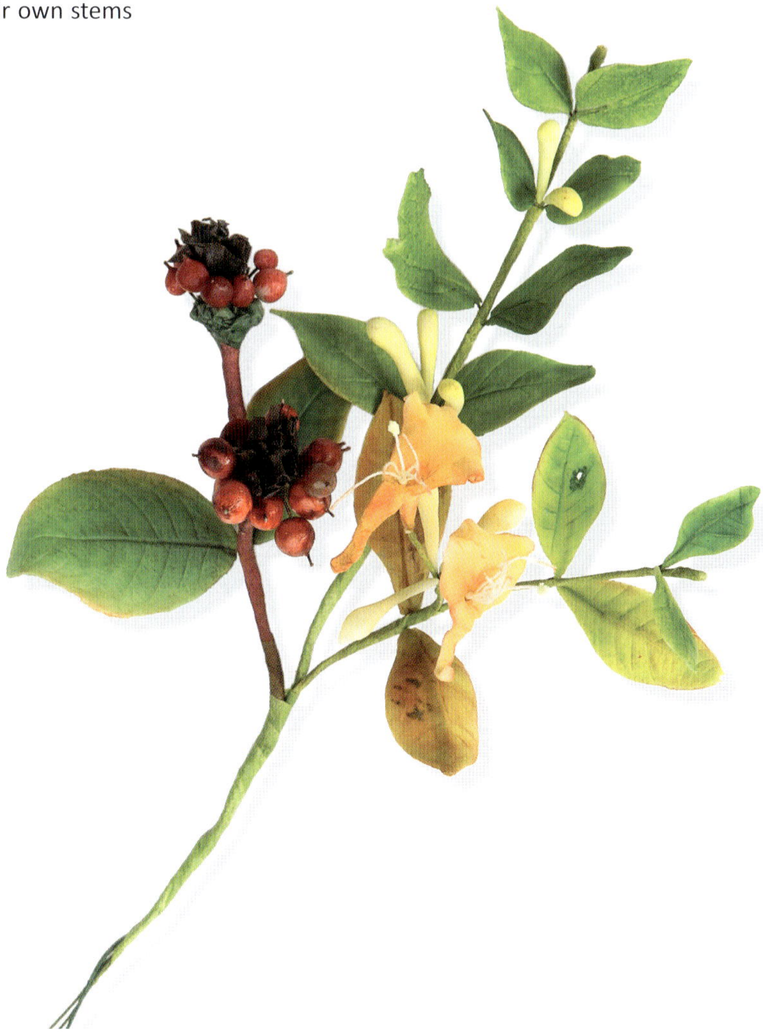

Story No. 6

Hypericum buds and berries - the calming effect

Hypericum berries form in various sizes, however their shape is pretty standard so they are easy to make. They are wonderful as fillers due to the assortment of colour which will add depth and character to many arrangements. Hot on the heels of the flower, the berry pops up as the petals fall. This plant, also known as the herbal 'pick me up' St Johns Wort, promotes a calming effect - and I've been known to have chewed a few leaves in my time.

Equipment

Arrowhead, ball tool and tweezers
Fine paint brush
5 petal calyx cutter (KB RO12)
Metal leaf cutters (FC 362 / set of 3)
Black bryony leaf veiner (SKGI - use the centre vein)

Materials

Pale green paste
28 gauge green wire - cut into 5 equal lengths
Half strength confectioners glaze or PME gloss spray varnish
Colour palette 1 & 2
Nile green or red florist tape ¼ and ½ width

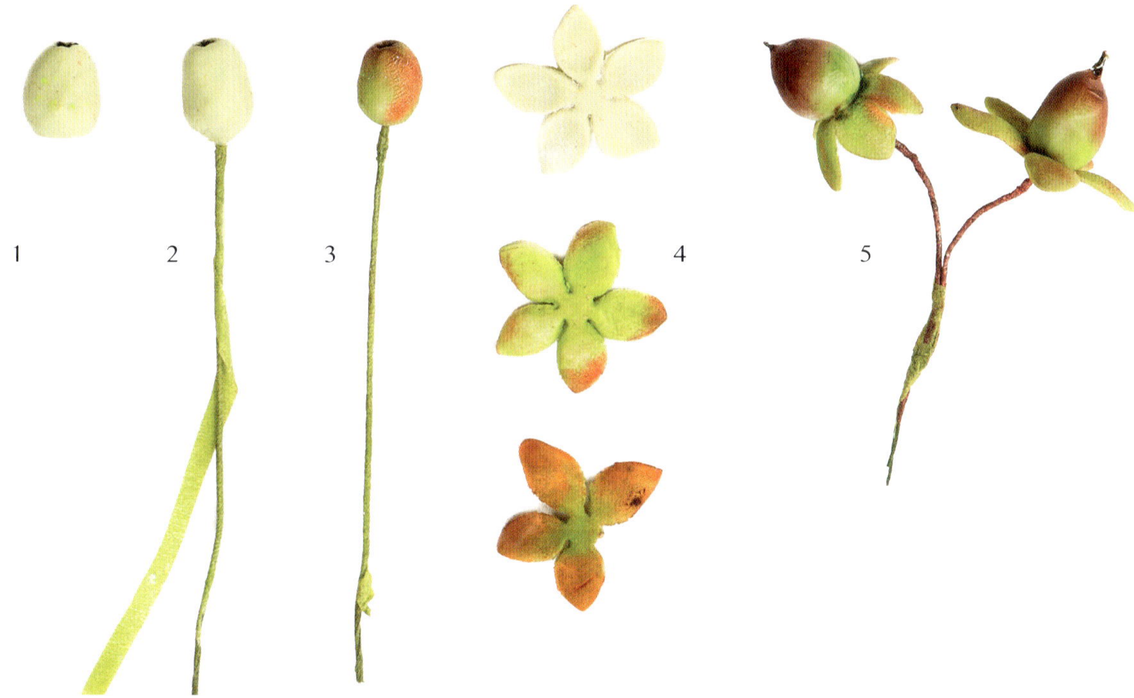

Berries

1. Roll an oval ball of green paste about the size of your little finger nail.

2. Insert a hooked 28g wire into the base and with an arrowhead tool make an indentation on the top of the berry. Mix with water or alcohol black/brown petals dust and dab into the indentation. Alternatively, insert a 28g wire up through the berry so it peeps out of the top. Tape the stem with ¼ width green tape.

3. Dust berries with a variation of spring green, moss, red and aubergine. The younger berries are almost all green with a touch of red and the older ones are a very dark aubergine. When dry varnish with ½ strength confectioners varnish or PME Edible Gloss spray

Calyx

4. Cut out a calyx from pale green paste to suit the size of your berry and gently soften the edges with a ball tool. Dust with colours to suit the matching berry, ie. light green and red around the edges for youngsters and green and terracotta for the more mature. Don't worry if you lose a petal off the calyx, it all adds to the flavour of nature.

5. Put a little glue on the bottom of the berry and insert the stem down through the centre of the calyx. Fold back the calyx to give shape. Leave the calyx matt and the glossy berry will stand proud. Lightly dust the tape of the stem with red to give interest and variation.

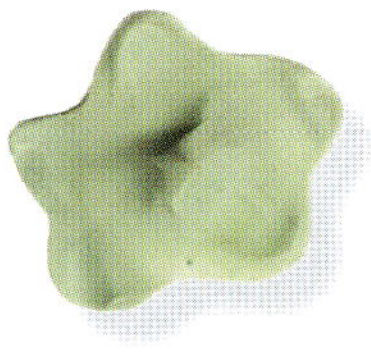

6

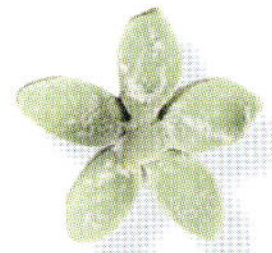

7

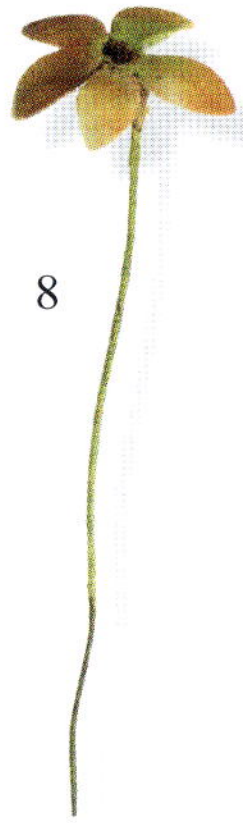

8

A single calyx

6. To make a calyx on its own, form a hat from green paste.

7. Cut out a calyx, soften the petals, cup each with a ball tool and insert a hooked wire down through the centre of the hat until it is hidden. With tweezers, pinch up a small rough circle in the centre.

8. Paint the circle with some terracotta and brown and dust the rest of the calyx with a mix of green and terra-cotta.

Leaves

9. Refer to the instructions on Pages 14-17.

10. Cut out leaves from pale green paste and use 26g wire cut into 4.

11. This leaf will come alive by dusting from the bottom centre up and out with a mixture of shades of green adding a touch of terracotta around the edges and in some places a splash of red. To give variation, make a small tear either on the edge or in the centre and dust the open sides with red.

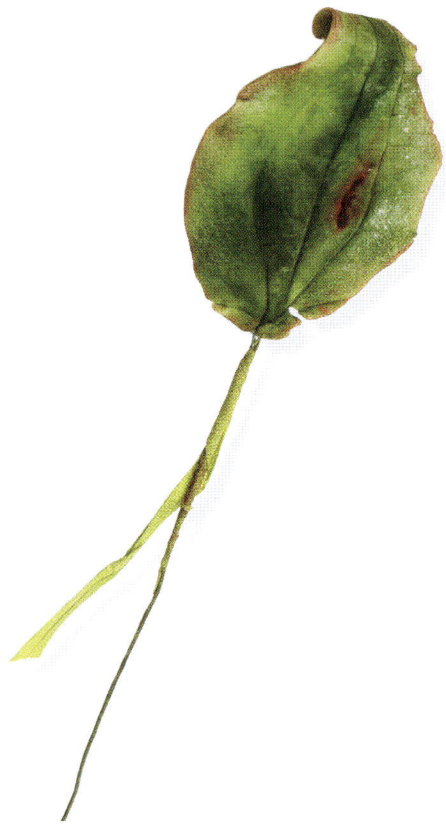

Assembly

12. Tape the berries together into groups of 5-7 varying the length of each berry onto a 24g wire. Group the leaves below in pairs. Make different sizes and shapes – fat round ones or some more pointed. Use lots of variation of colour to bring depth and interest when included into sprays.

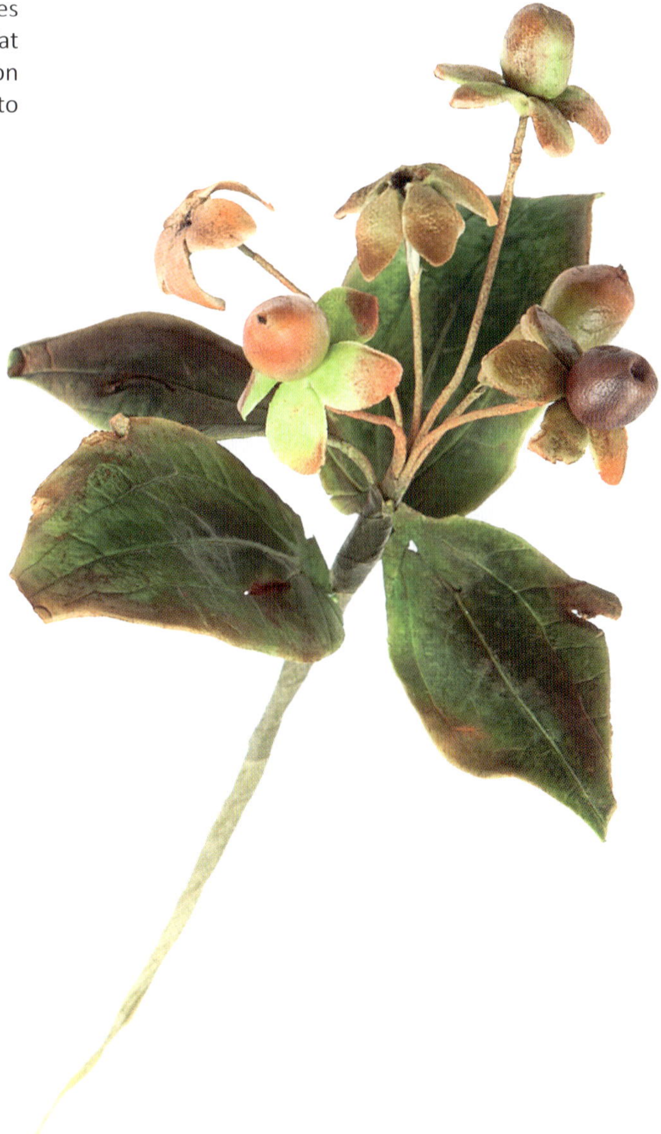

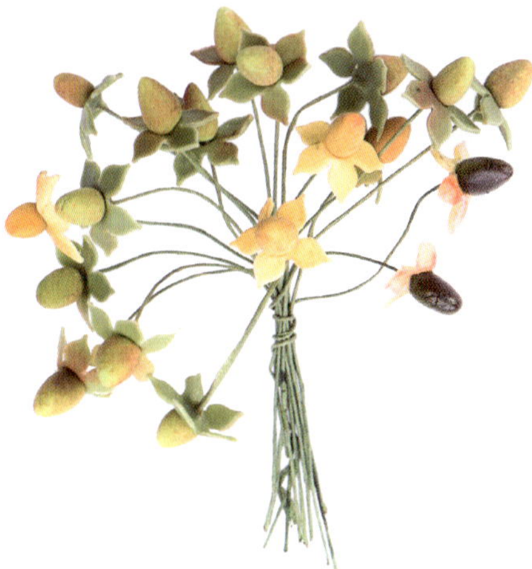

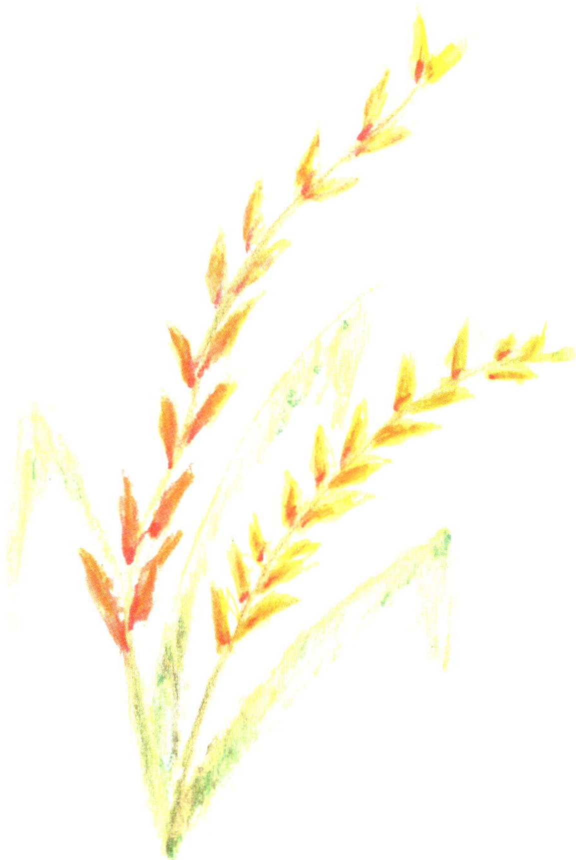

Story No. 7

Monbretia stems - slim and elegant (in my dreams!)

Swaying gently in the breeze, the tall Monbretia flowering stems emerge from their mass of sturdy foliage in a blaze of orange and red reminding me why I keep this overgrowing plant in the flowerbed. Quite a striking flower and almost abstract in form it is worthy of inclusion in many floral arrangements.

Equipment

Cel stick
Small scissors
Dusting brush for colour
5 Petal calyx cutter (FC 165 / set of 3)

Materials

Pale Yellow paste
24, 28 & 30g wire
Colour palette 2
Nile green florist tape
Small stamens

Monbretia stems - slim and elegant (in my dreams!)

Buds

1. Cut each 30g wire into 6 pieces. Roll a small ball of pale yellow paste between your fingers into a long thin tear drop. Insert the wire into the narrow end and very lightly pinch the top to bring it to a soft point.

2. Make a couple of dozen for each stem in different sizes.

3. On the bigger buds, with scissors make two snips at opposite sides on the bottom of the bud – this will act as a mini calyx.

4. Dust up with oranges, reds and yellows, blending the colours to be smooth, deeper at the base by the wire and ending with yellow at the tip. Dust the tiny calyx at the bottom with light green.

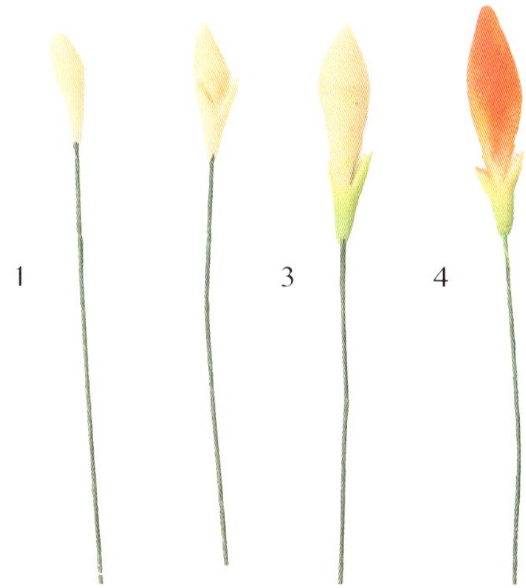

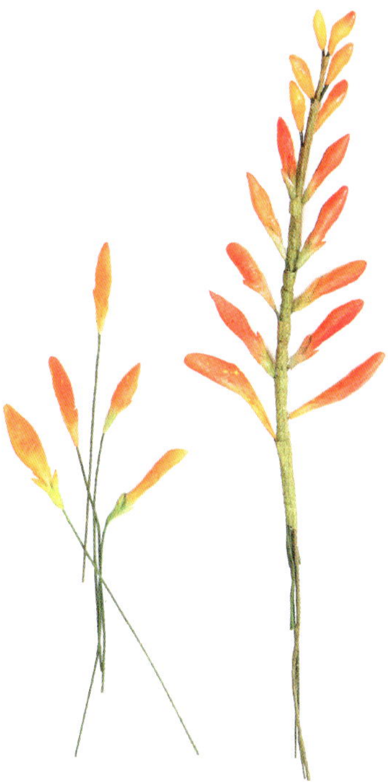

Bud Stems

5. With ¼ width nile green tape, attach the buds onto both sides of the 24g wire. To start with the buds are quite close together, however as they move down the stem they become further apart.

Blooms

6. Tape 3 small white stamens to a 28g wire.

7. Roll out a hat of yellow paste place the calyx cutter over the hat and cut out. Turn the flower over and place the tail between your first and middle finger. Gently soften the edges of each petal with either your fingers or a ball tool.

8. Hollow the centre with a cel stick. Carefully dust with oranges and reds with a slightly lighter yellow around the centre.

9. Insert the wired stamens down through the middle. Twist the stem gently between your fingers to secure. Open up the petals to achieve the desired shape.

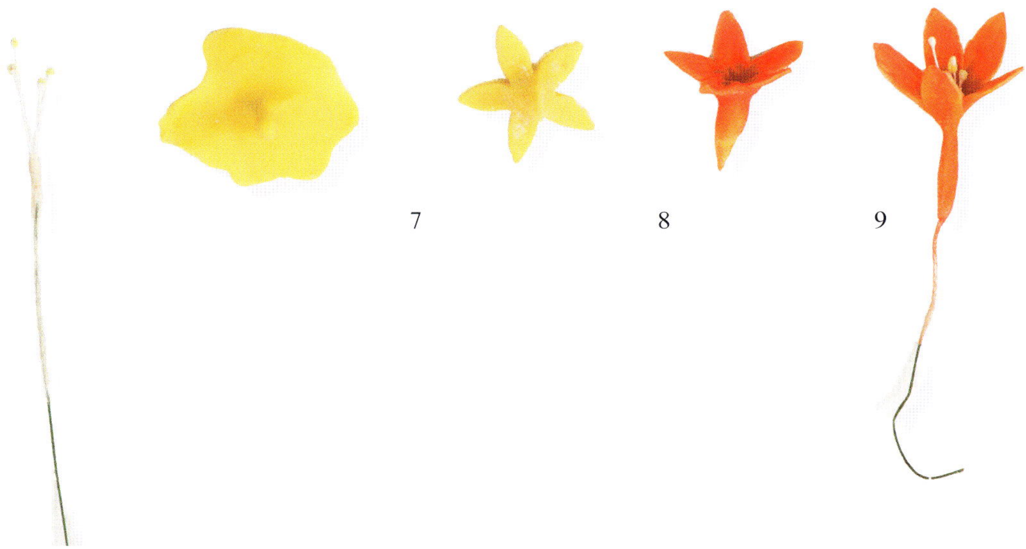

6 7 8 9

Assembly

10. Follow step 3 adding the flowers towards the bottom of the stem. Use ¼ width tape. The wires should be enough to support the stem however if making a long stem you may need to add in a 22g or 24g wire as you move down the stem to increase the strength.

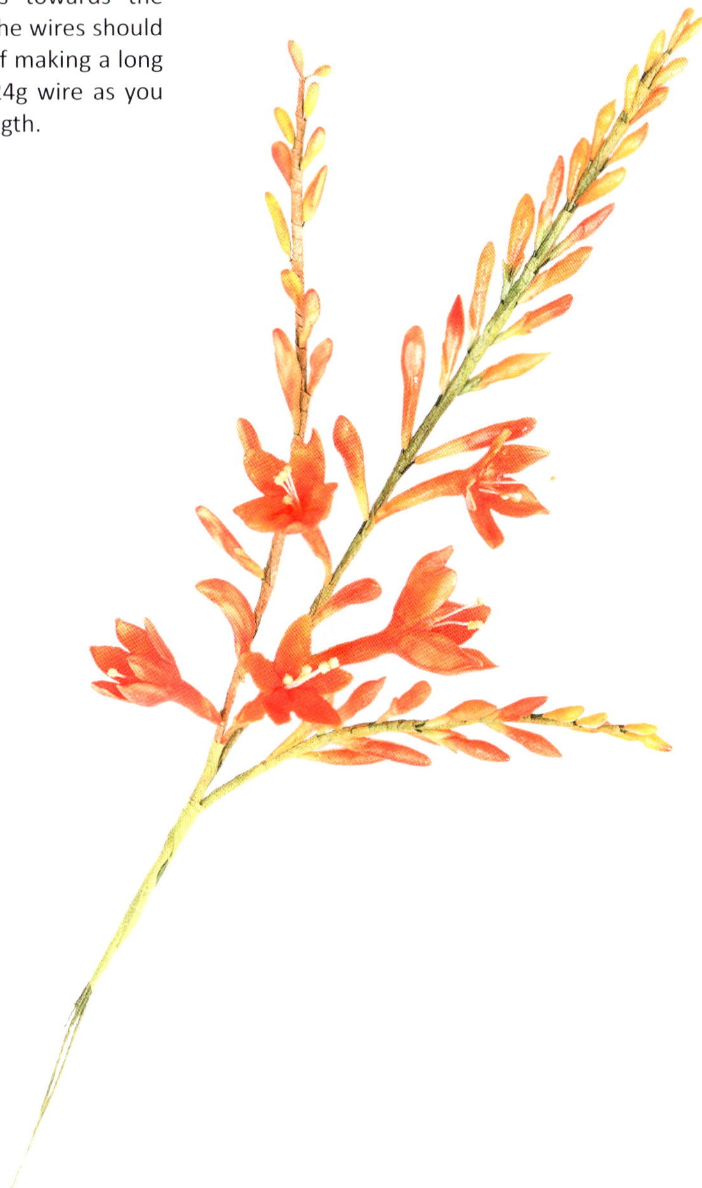

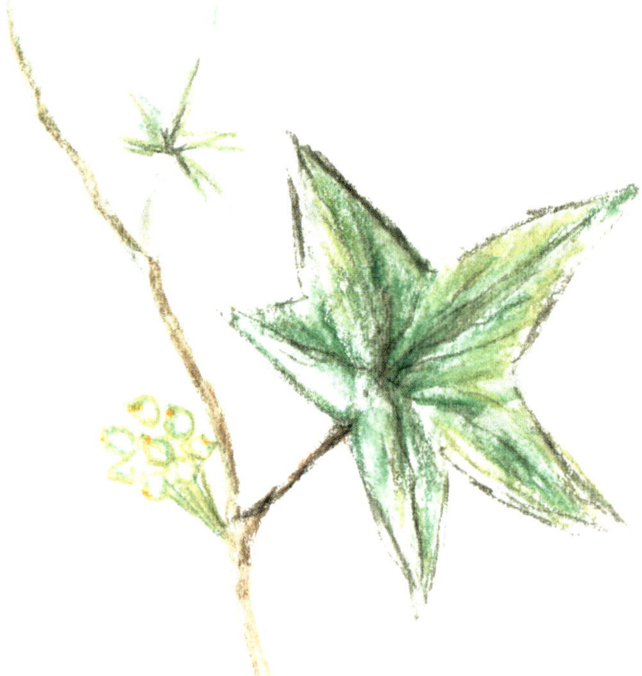

Story No. 8

Ivy leaves and berries – holding it all together

Strolling past the hedgerows, I find myself surprised by the number of variations of ivy there are. Not only different in shape and colour, but some with fabulous berries, which remind me of the metal Jacks we used to play with at school. The dilemma now is that we are spoilt for choice but in return it gives us the opportunity to mix and match both trailing and bush examples to either compliment other flowers or to make a display of their own.

Equipment

Ivy leaf cutters (TT metal cutter set 45-60mm)
Plastic cutter plunger set (PME)
Ivy leaf cutter (KB Size 3 R034, Size 2 R033 & Size 1 R032)
Birdsfoot ivy leaf veiner (SKGI)

Materials

22, 24, 26 & 28g wire
Pale green or cream paste
Colour palette 1
PME gloss spray or ½ strength confectioners varnish
Brown pollen
Ball point pen or similar

Berries

1. Roll a small pea size ball of pale green paste and insert a 28g wire. Leave the majority of the paste in a ball at the top and roll the rest between finger and thumb down the wire about 25mm. With the plastic circle point of a ball point pen – nib retracted, imprint a small circle onto the tip. Dust with pale greens and lightly dab brown over so it looks like speckles. Make 15-20.

2. Repeat above, but with a bigger pea size ball and roll the paste down the wire about 40mm. Dust with darker greens. Put a little glue on the tip and dip into brown pollen. Lightly dust a little terrcotta over the pollen. Make 9 to 12.

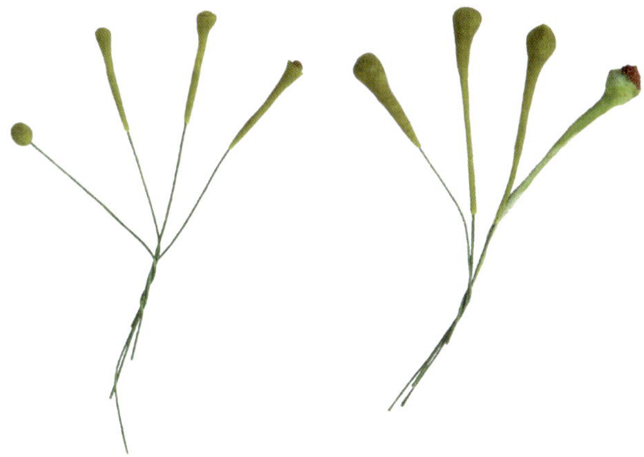

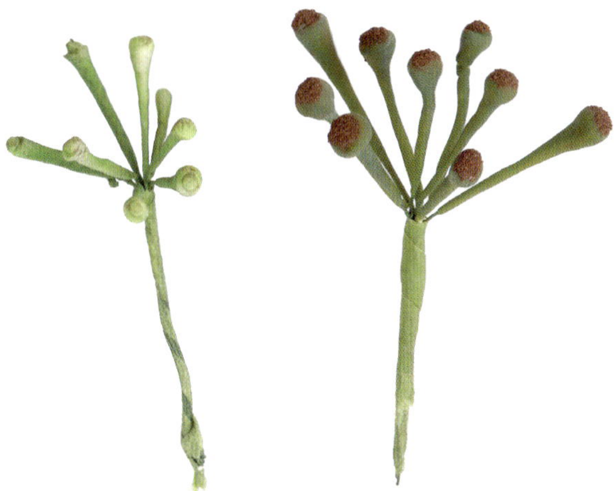

3. Group the smaller berries together in batches of 7 to 9 and tape with ½ width nile green tape. With tweezers or fine pliers, pull each berry out and spread apart. Do the same with the larger berries making one large group.

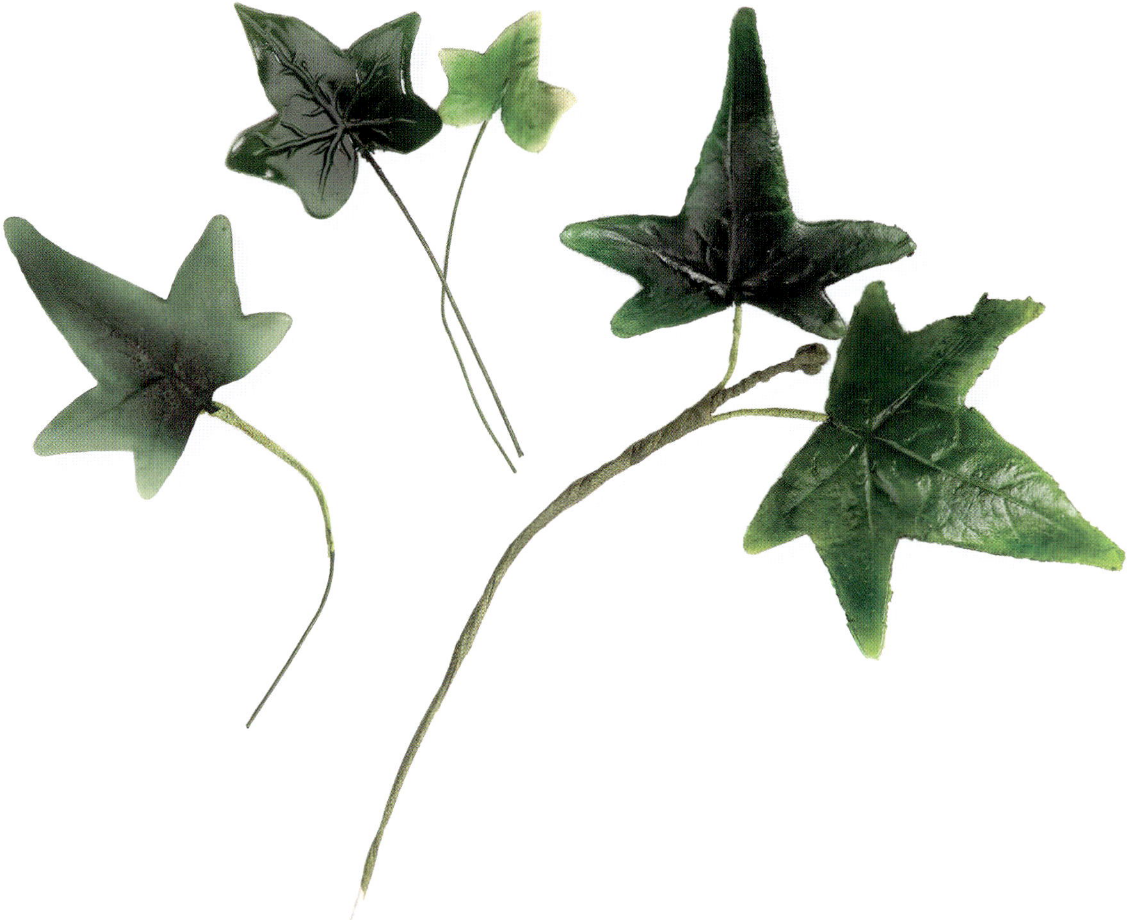

Leaves

4. Refer to the instructions on Pages 14-17.

5. Use 26 & 28g wire cut into 5. Make leaves of various sizes. Experiment with your colouring and vary the shades. This will not look out of place as it will show the leaves in all stages of growth. When dry, varnish with PME gloss spray or dip in ½ strength glaze.

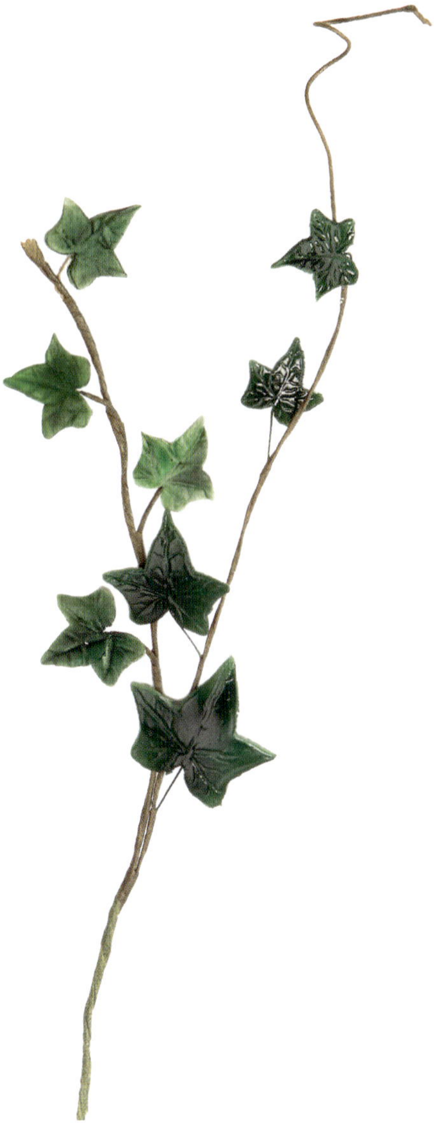

Assembly

6. For trailing ivy, tape over the top and 75mm down a 24g wire with ½ width brown or beige florist tape. Start adding leaves with the smallest first on alternate sides and at regular intervals, with the leaves gradually increasing in size as you move down the stem. Curl the top end of the wire loosely around a cel stick to give the impression of new growth.

7. For the bush ivy, attach the large berry group to the top of a 22g wire adding the 2 groups of smaller berries down the stem at approximately 25mm intervals and on alternate sides. Add the leaves around the stem OR make 2 or 3 smaller separate stems with different amounts of leaves and berries.

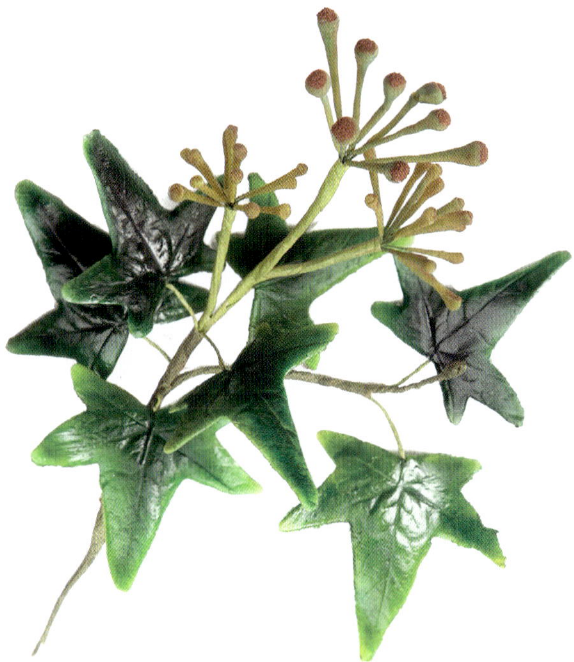

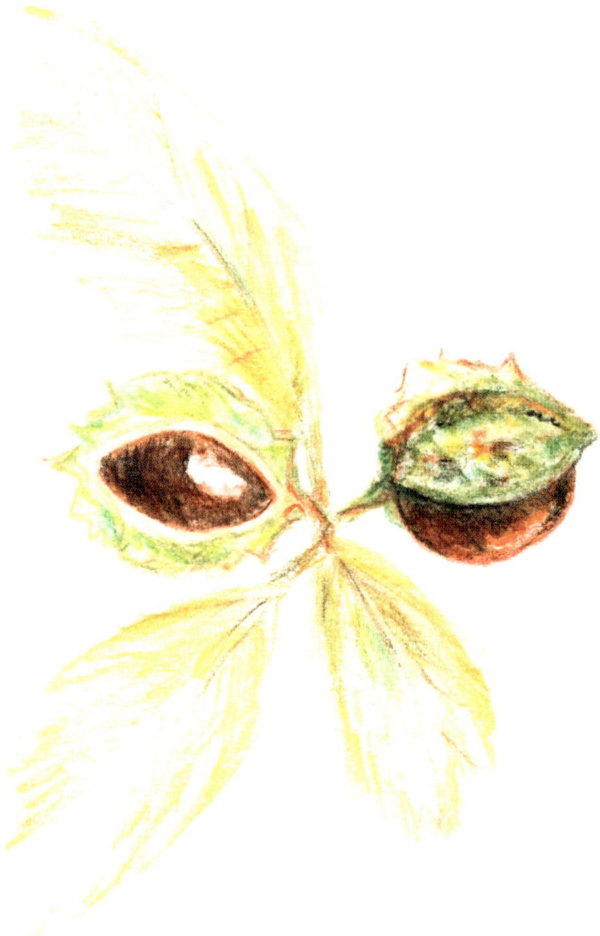

Story No. 9

Conkers and Horse Chestnut leaves – reminds me of my childhood

Armed with a ball of string and a skewer, as children we would gather under the Horse Chestnut tree in the school playground, hunting for conkers to transform them into champion weapons. I can't tell you the number of bruises I had on my hands, but I still remember the pain as my opponents conker smashed down on my knuckles!

Equipment

Scalpel
Cel stick
Ball tool
Cutting wheel or circle cutter (FC Circle 1850)
Horse chestnut leaf cutter (KB Set 0135)
Horse chestnut leaf veiner (SKGI medium)

Materials

White, pale green and cream paste
20, 26 & 24g wires
Colour palette 1 & 2
Green and beige florist tape
Confectioners varnish full glaze

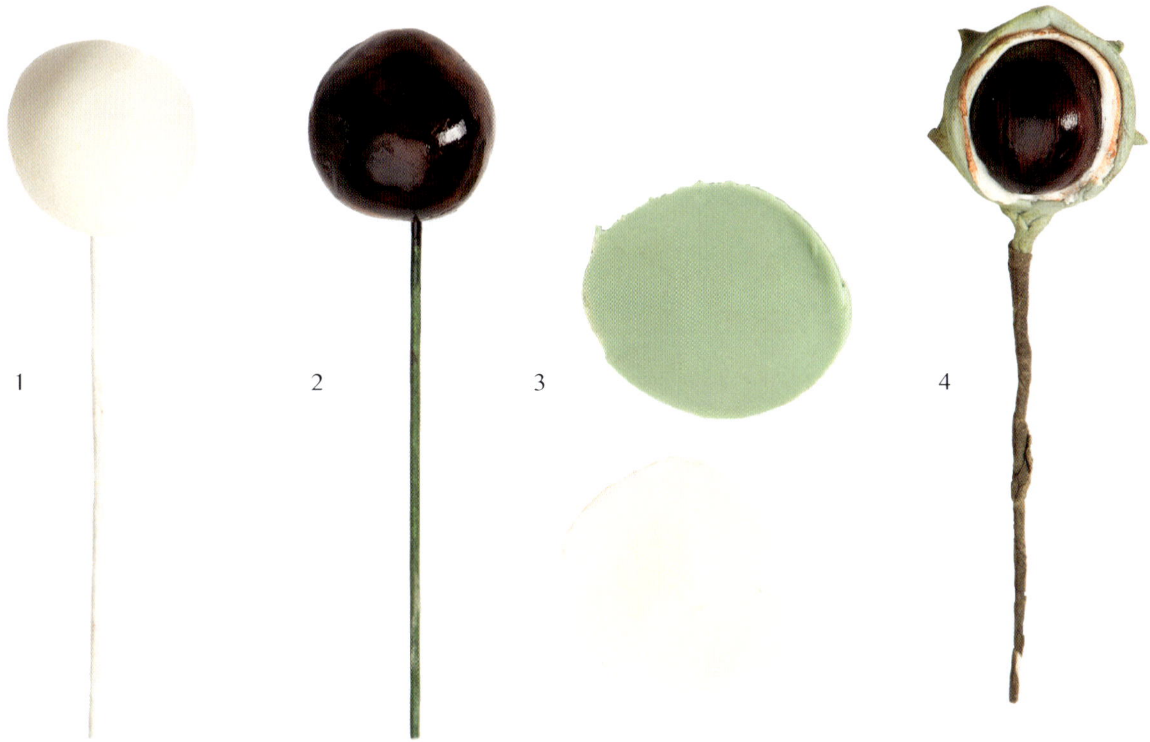

Conkers

1. In advance roll 3 balls of white paste about the size of a new 10p coin (24mm). Insert a hooked 20g wire and leave to dry upright. Paint half the ball in a chestnut brown colour.

2. When dry dip into confectioner's varnish to get a lovely glossy shine. Leave to dry.

3. Roll out and cut a circle of white paste about 2mm thick large enough to wrap ½ to ¾ around the ball. Lightly glue and wrap it around the coloured ball like a bonnet. Cut out a circle of green paste the same size, glue and lay it over the white paste. Pinch down the back of the chestnut with your thumb and forefinger to create a ridge. Then pinch the porcelain together, creating little raised spikes over the chestnut on either side of the ridge.

4. Using a scalpel, gently cut away a neat edge around the open face. With a fine brush, paint a thin brown line along the join between the white and the green porcelain to emphasise the different layers.

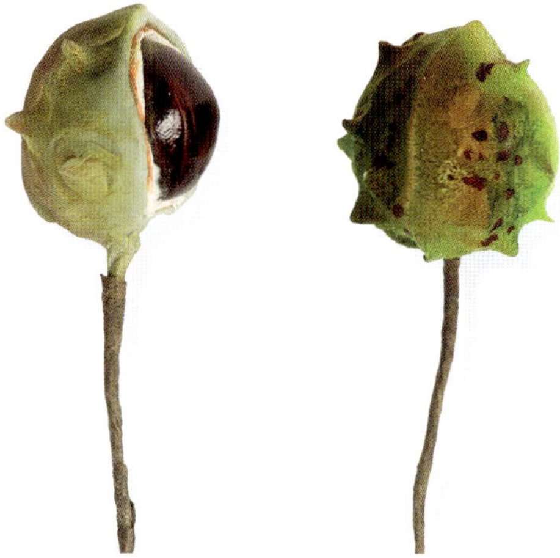

5. Dust with a mixture of greens, yellow and brown. To vary, paint dark brown spots onto the conker shell and tape the stem with beige florist tape.

Leaves

6. Refer to the instructions on Pages 14-17.

7. Use 26g wire unless you intend to make a whopper. In that case use a thicker wire.

8. From cream paste cut out the shape of the leaf either with the cutter or freehand. Gently pull and scrape around the edge of the leaf giving it a slightly crumpled look. If bits tear don't worry as these will look fabulous when you start to colour.

9. Using a mixture of greens, yellows and orange, give life to your leaf by starting at the base with the greens, darker in the centre, slowly shading in the yellows and ending up with the orange towards the outer edges of the leaf. Take the flat side of the brush and rub that along the edge of the leaf to highlight the snags you made earlier and add to the character. Make a couple of small holes in the leaf and brush these edges in the same way. Looks like something's nibbled.

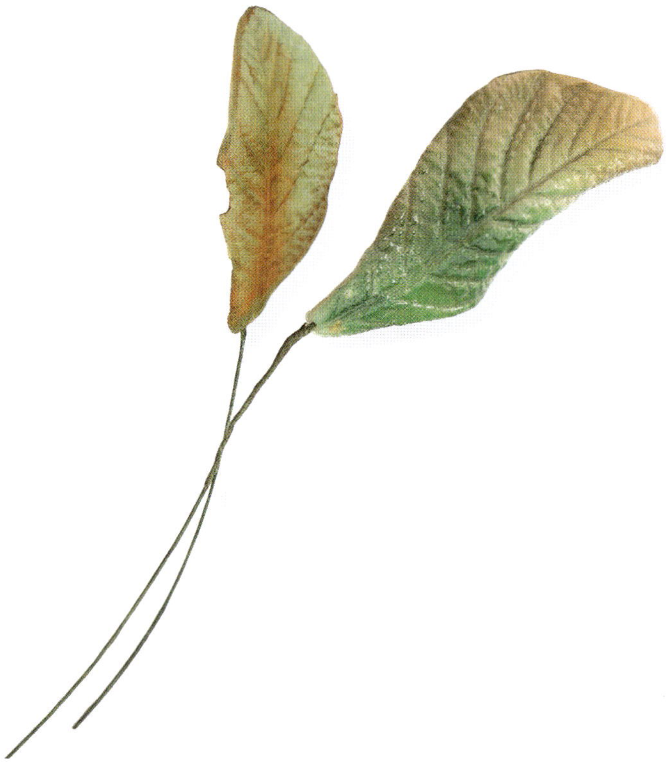

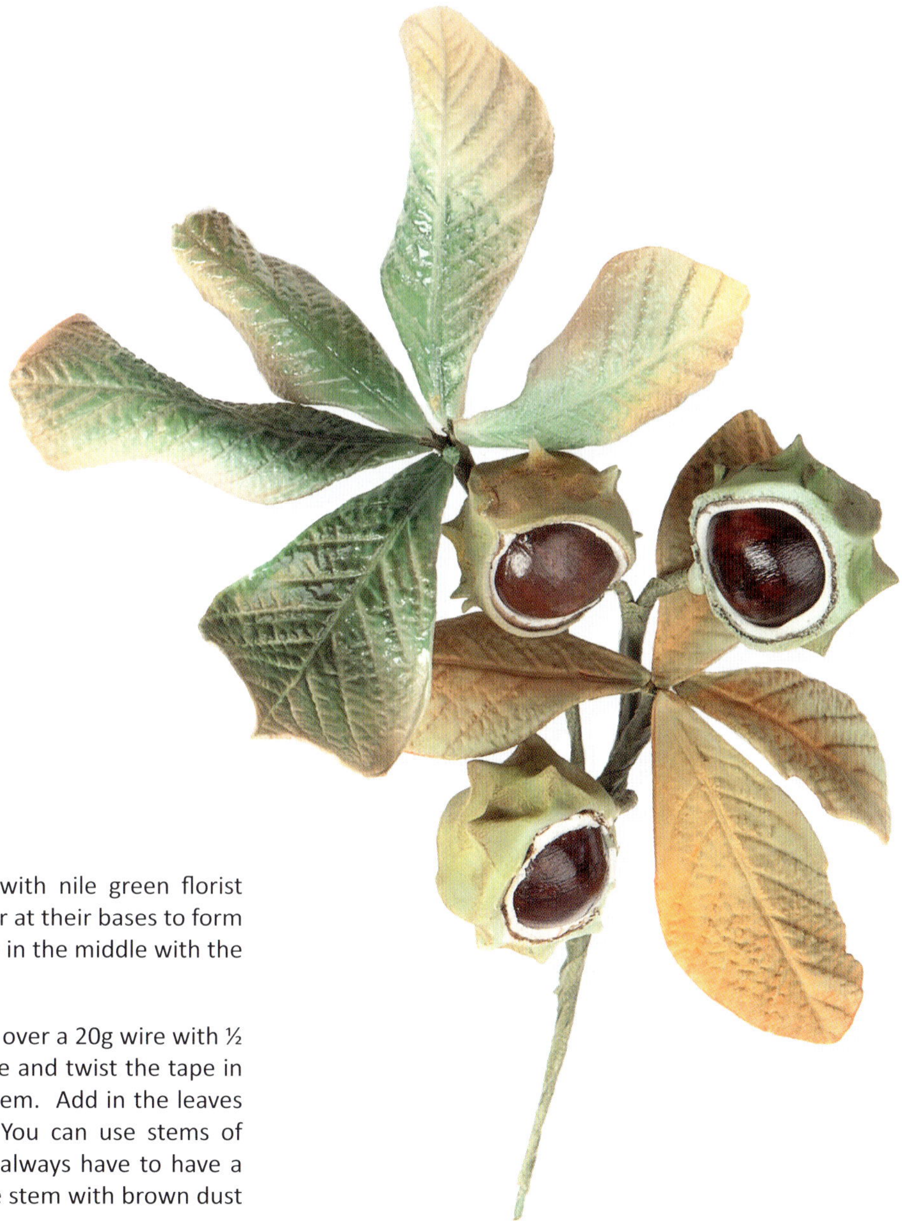

Assembly

10. Tape down each leaf stem with nile green florist tape. Tape 5 leaves tightly together at their bases to form a fan shape. The largest leaves are in the middle with the smallest on the outside.

11. To make the main stem, tape over a 20g wire with ½ width green florist tape. Over tape and twist the tape in places to make 'nobbles' on the stem. Add in the leaves and conkers where you see fit. You can use stems of leaves on their own, they do not always have to have a conker on them. Lightly colour the stem with brown dust to give interest.

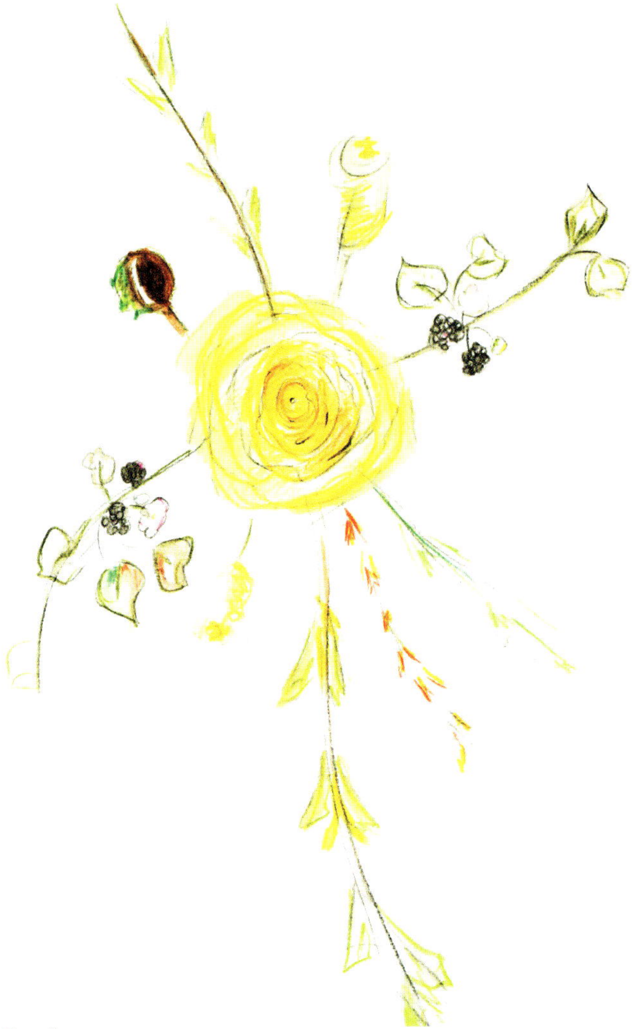

Guidance on assembly

At the bottom of each Story page there is a picture showing how the flowers have been taped into a stem. This is only a guide, you can make the stems any size and any shape. Use your artistic licence.

The hardest part of putting together an arrangement is getting started. Make a sketch of the basic shape you would like to create - mine resembles a slightly wonky cross (see left). Make sure you tape the stems tightly together so they will not 'swing' away from each other. Use florist wire to give extra strength on larger arrangements. Once you have secured the four main points of the shape, the rest takes care of itself.

It is not always necessary to tape each individual wire separately before being over taped securely to the stem. However a small amount of ¼ width tape on 28g or 30g wires will help secure the leaf or berry in place by sticking to the main wire of the stem and prevent it becoming loose.

This style of arrangement will look terrific across a piece of driftwood and placed in the centre of the table for all to admire.

Equipment

A selection of 22, 20 & 18g wires in case you need to increase the length or strength of stems
Pliers for cutting and positioning stems or individual flowers
Thin Florist wire
Florist tape cutter

To make an arrangement similar to the one being demonstrated you will need the flowers listed below. It will depend on the size and the length of the made up stems of your flowers as to how many you will need and how they will fit together. I have listed the number of stems included in this spray, which is quite open, but would suggest you make some extra to play with as it is better to have too many to use rather than too few to fill the spray. You can use any leftover flowers to make something else.

- 5 roses with 3 sets of leaves
- 3 rose hips plus leaves
- 3 stems of honeysuckle leaves and flowers – one stem approximately 200mm long and two stems 125-150mm in length
- 1 smaller stem of the honeysuckle berries
- 2 stems of blackberries and flowers – vary size
- 1 stem of Monbretia bud and flowers
- 3 stems of varied hypericum berries
- 1 stem of acorns and oak leaves
- 3 stems of ivy – again, one longer and you can just use a couple of large ivy leaves and add a few simple berries as well
- 1 small horse chestnut with a selection of leaves

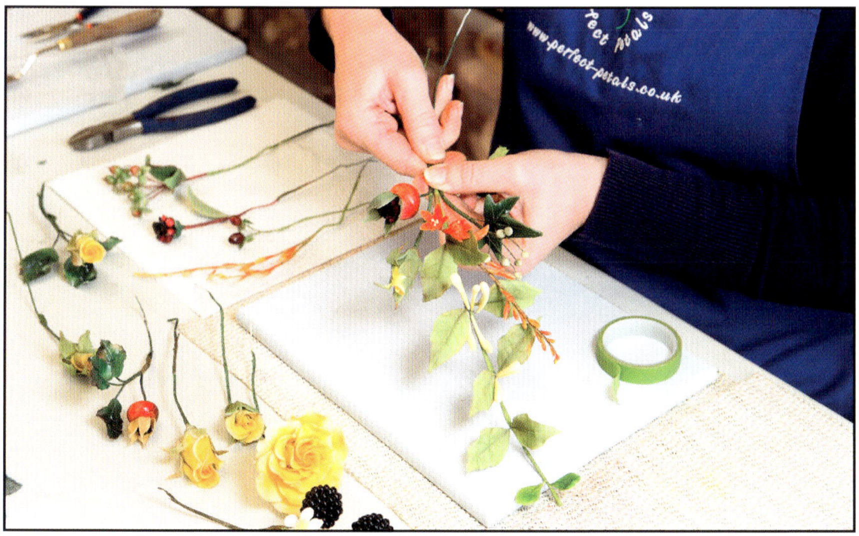

Assembly

1. Lay out your stems of flowers on the table so you can see their individual shapes and sizes. To begin, hold your longest stem of honeysuckle (or perhaps ivy) and position 2-3 stems of other flowers around it, holding them altogether at the base and leaving the longest length to the honeysuckle. Here I have used a rose, rosehip, a stem of Monbretia and a single ivy leaf with simple berries.

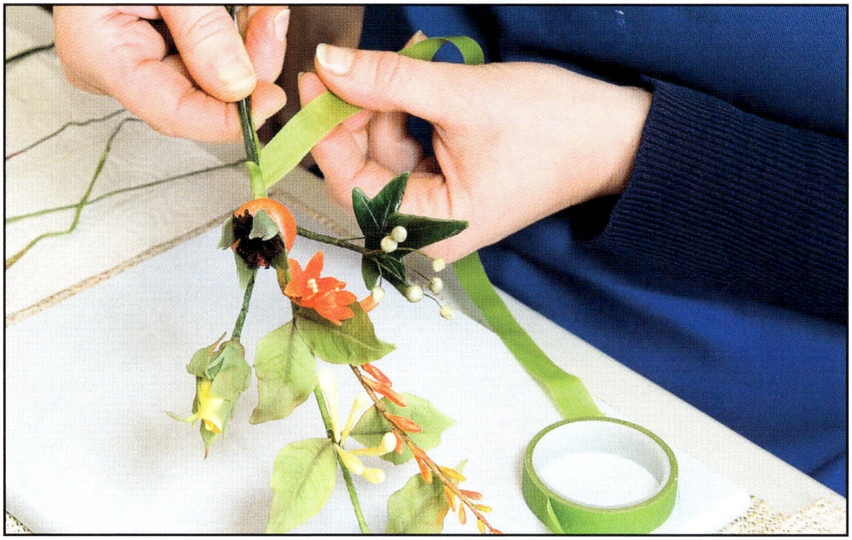

2. Tape the stems together at the same point to create one main individual stem. Taping the flowers at one point will give strength. This creates the lower half of the cross.

3. Add in two sprays of blackberries of similar but not equal lengths to create the centre cross piece. Attach with green tape/wire both pieces into the same place on the first stem. Add in your central rose, slightly raised and proud (so you will be able to put other flowers in underneath). Tape a second honeysuckle stem between the longest stem and blackberries on the lower right.

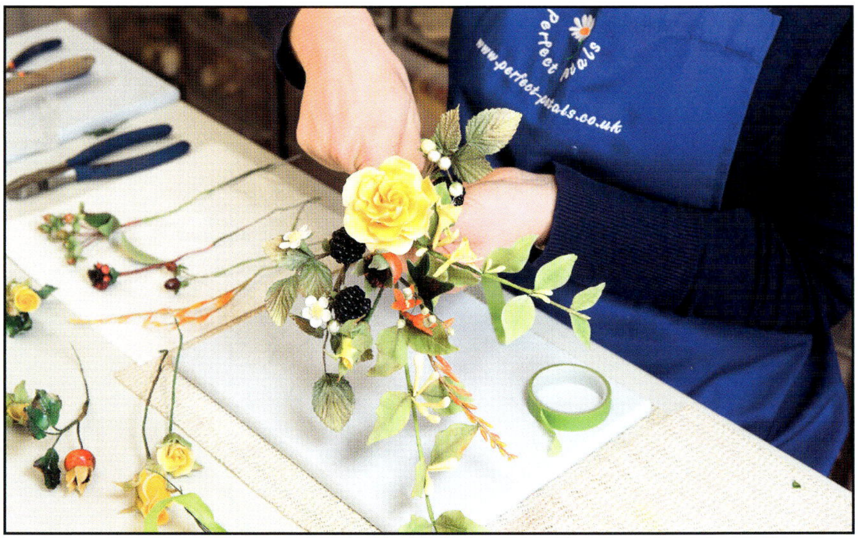

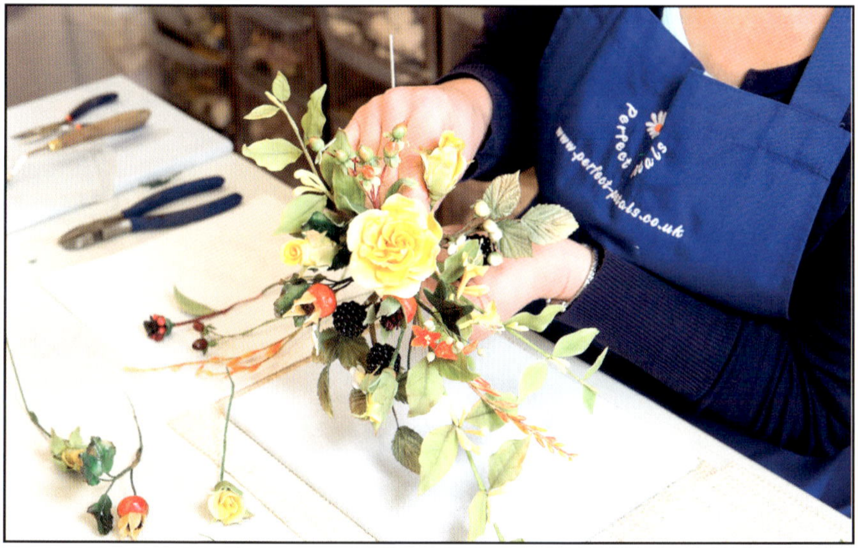

4. Now add in the top piece of honeysuckle, taping as close to the original point as possible and bend it backwards into position slightly left of centre (top left facing the spray) to balance with the second honeysuckle stem which is at the bottom right. Position and tape in flowers to fill between the 4 points, but extending no further than the cross pieces to avoid losing the shape.

5. Fill in the spaces around the central rose. Try different flowers to see which ones fit best. All these flowers will look fabulous together in any order, but it is their shapes which will dictate where they will be more comfortably placed.

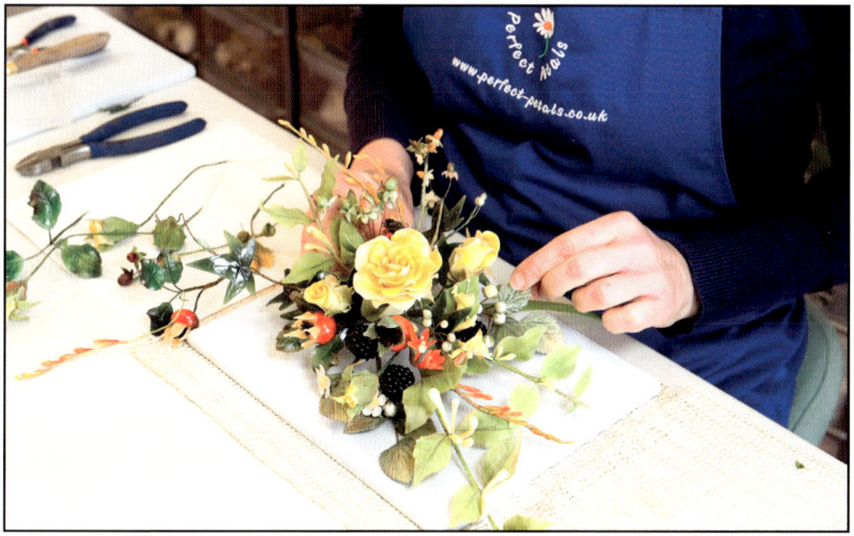

6. When you are happy with the design of your arrangement, and nearing completion position it the way you intend to display and check to see how it looks overall. Cut the wires as appropriate, fully taping down the stem to finish off.

7. Now leave the room for 5 minutes – do something completely different – then come back in and with fresh eyes look at what you have made. Wow!

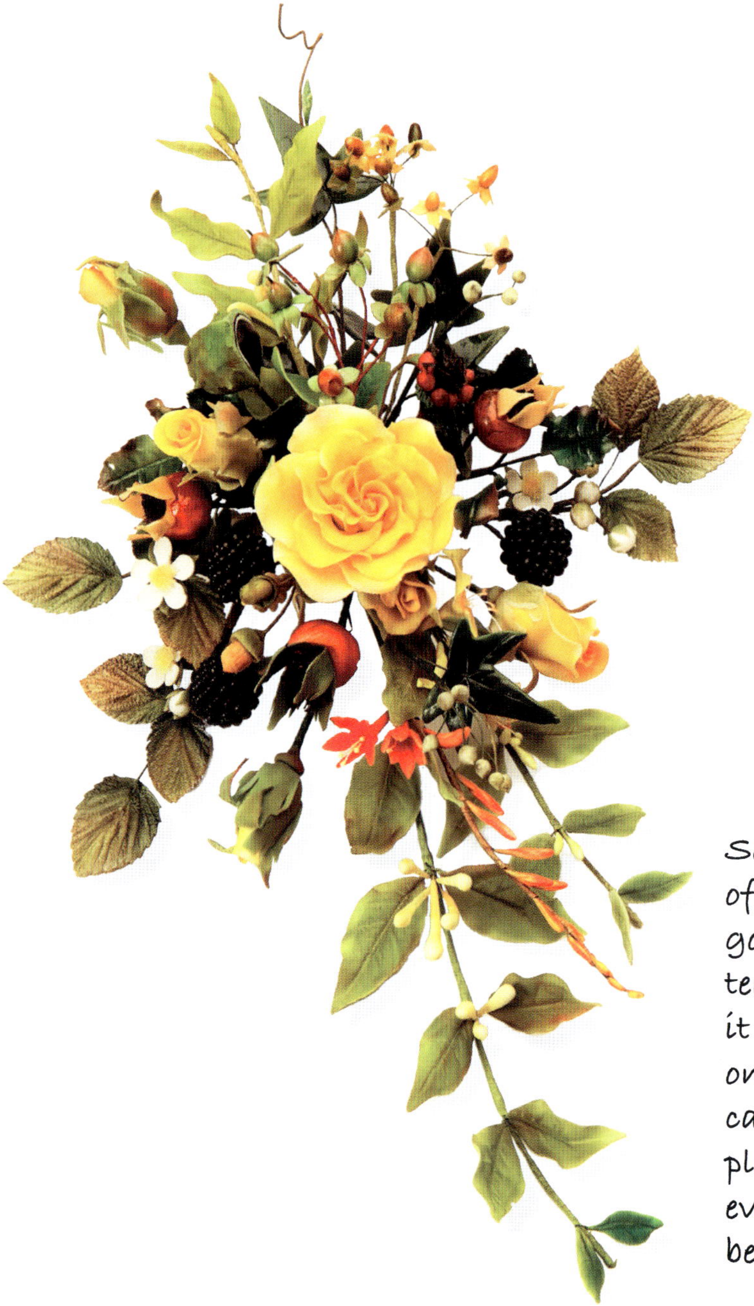

Sometimes human nature has a habit of making us feel that no matter how good we may become at something, we tend to believe someone else could do it better. The fact remains that each one of us can only ever be the best we can be on that particular day. So take pleasure and pride in what you create every day, because no one else will have been able to make it quite like you.

Final story

To help you on your way, here are some photographs to inspire you with ideas of what you can do with the lovely flowers within this book that you have made. Small or large, the choice is yours.

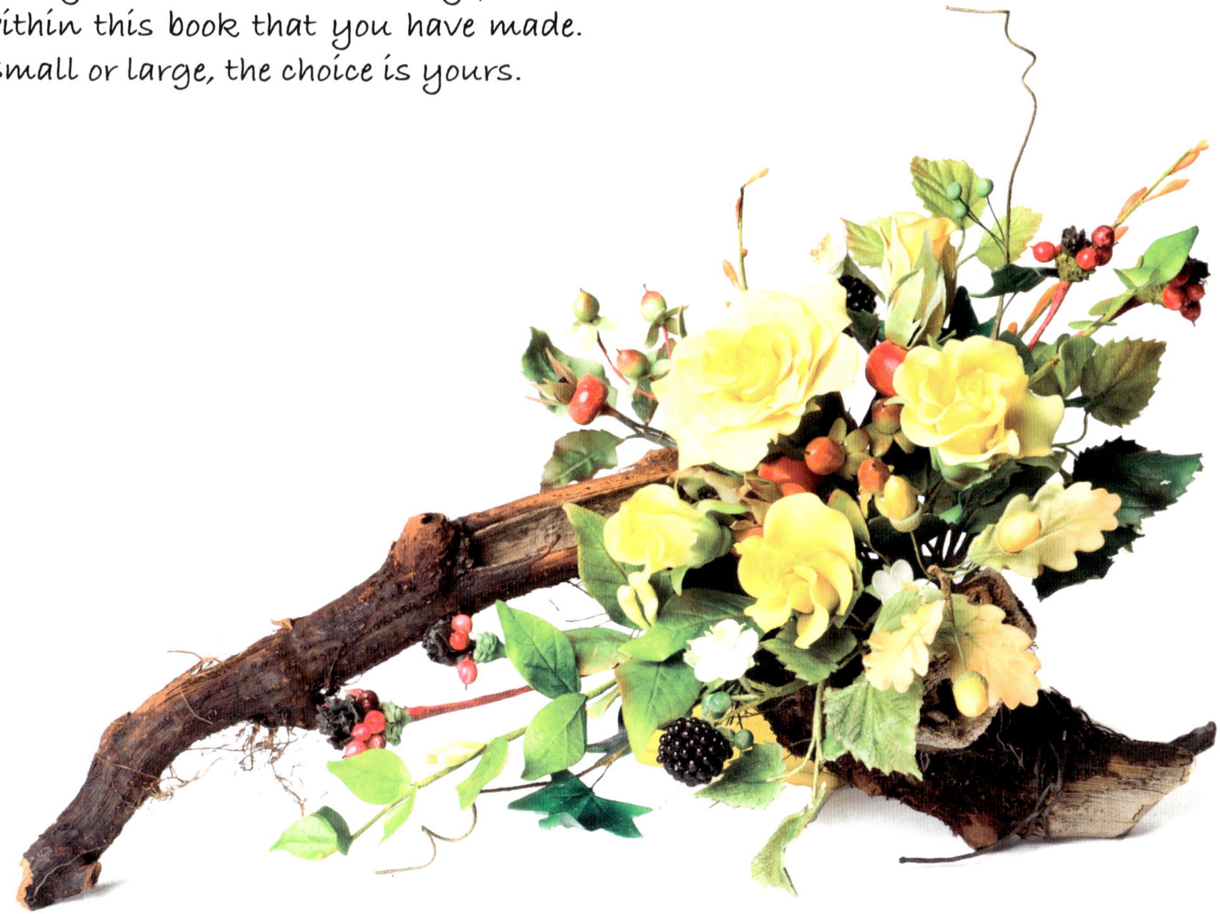

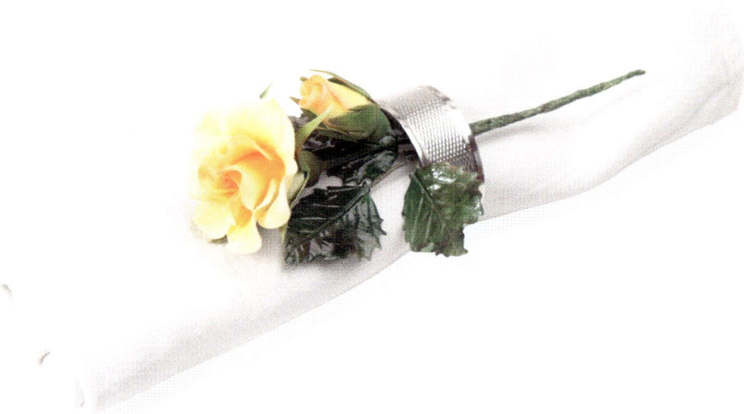

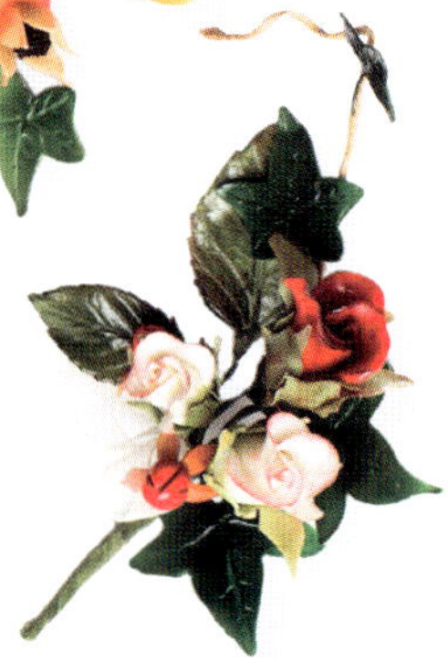

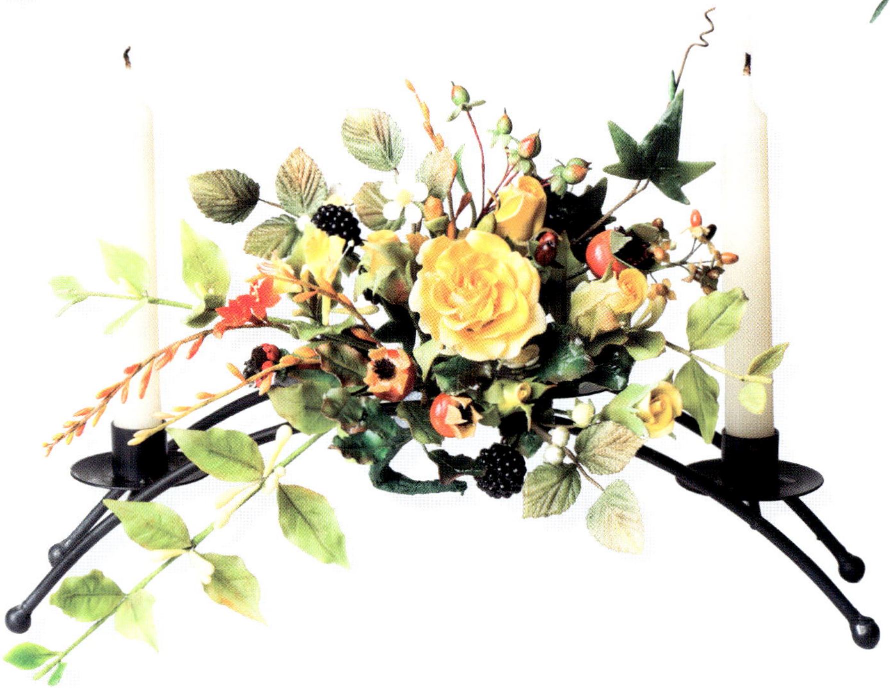

From table decorations and corsages ....

.... to gift tags, candles and cakes

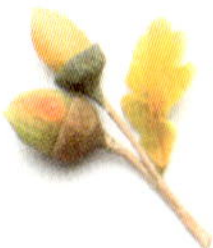

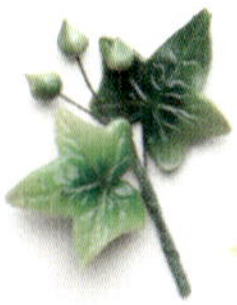

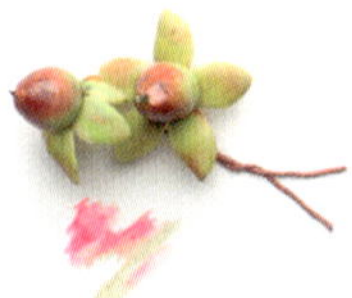

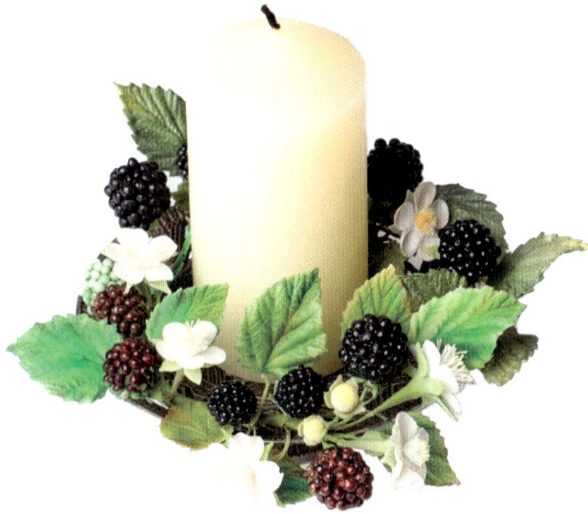

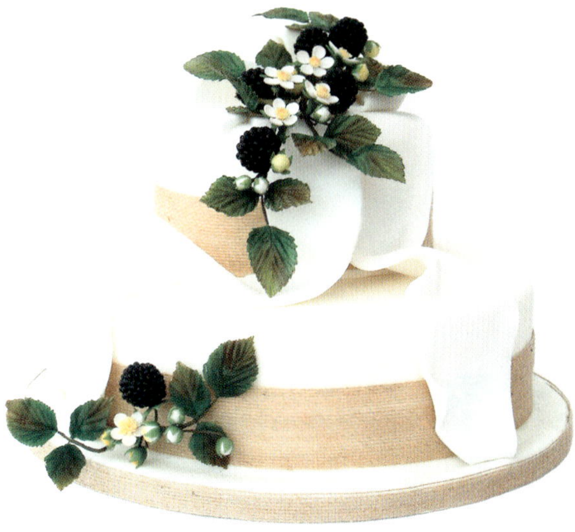

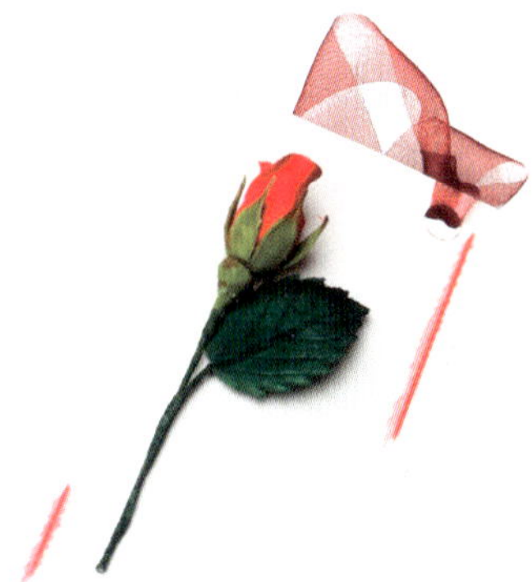

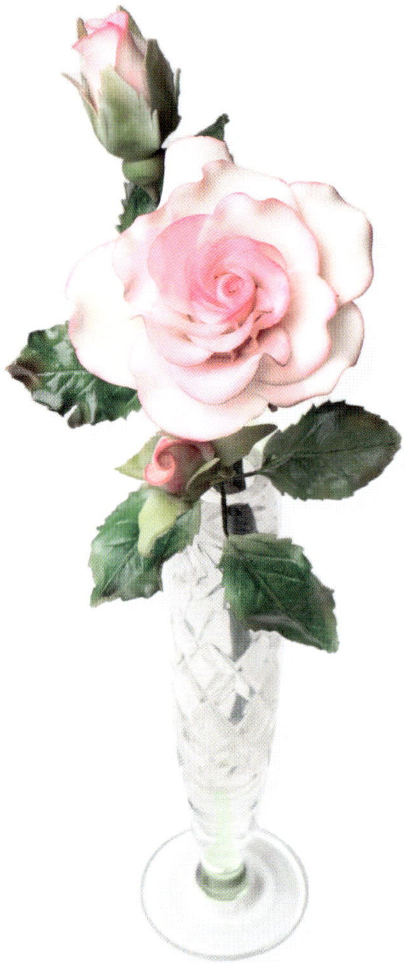

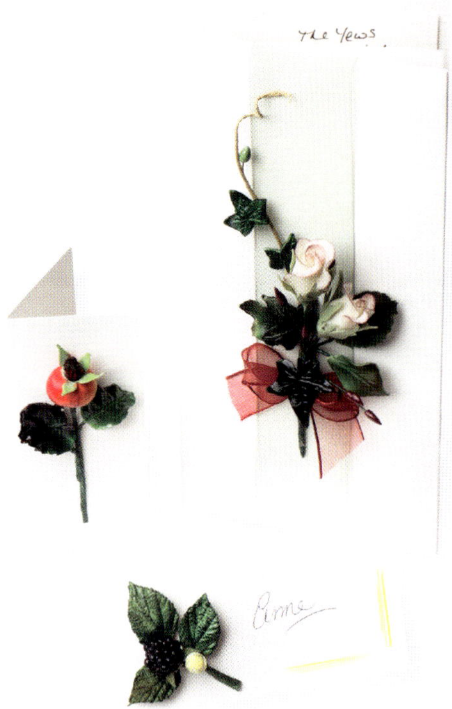

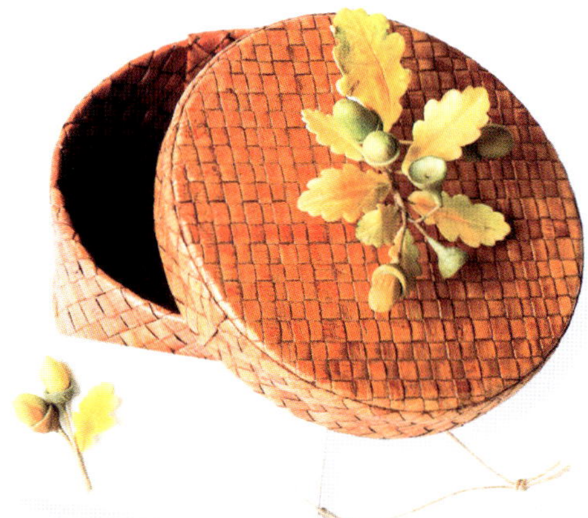

From dressing table and special gifts ....

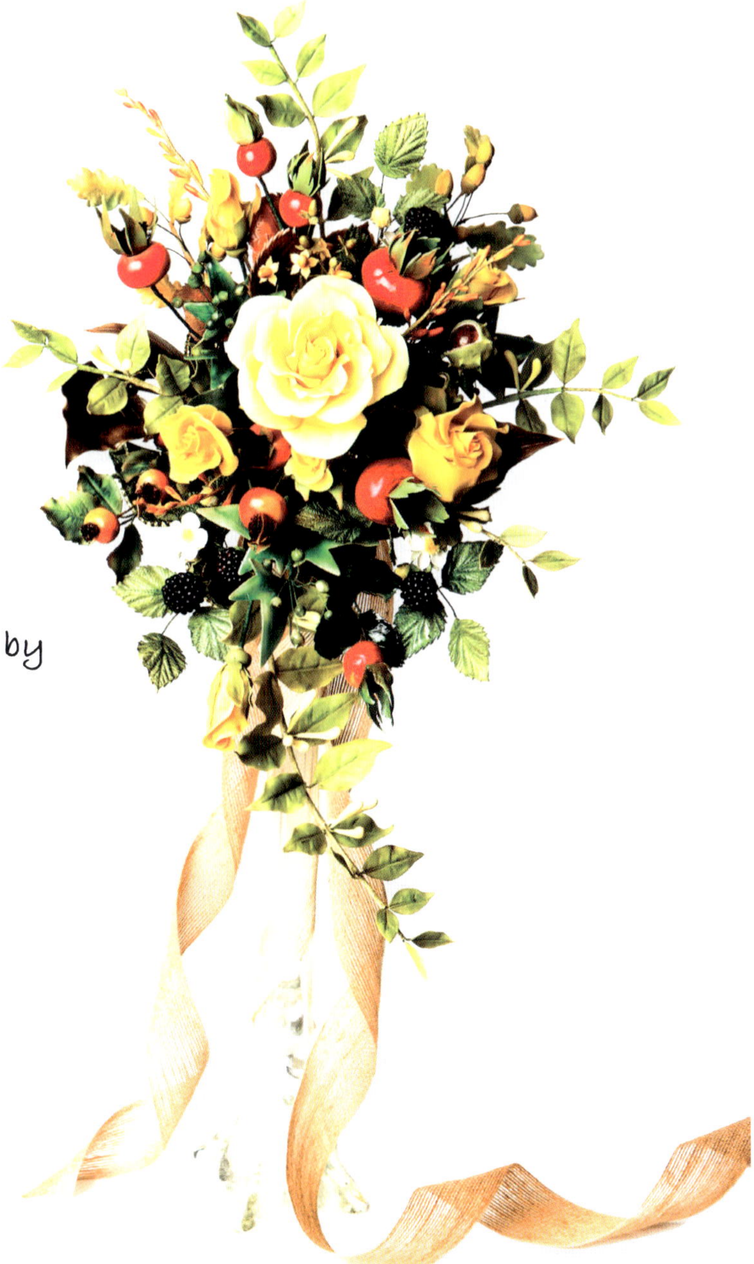

.... to lasting memories of days gone by

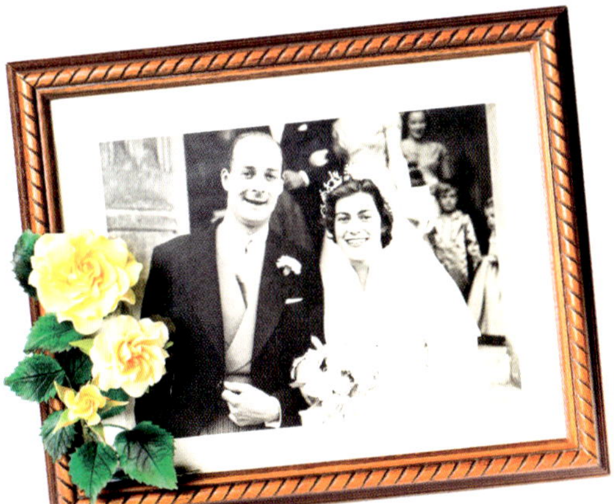

Cutters and veiners

Roses & Rose Hips

There are many cutters and veiners available from a number of specialist suppliers to help make these projects a little easier. Alternatively, you can use a scalpel or cutting wheel to cut out the various leaves, calyxes and petals by hand – size and shape to suit you. Here are examples of some of the cutters and veiners I have used within this project. Some of these cutters have been used on different flowers.

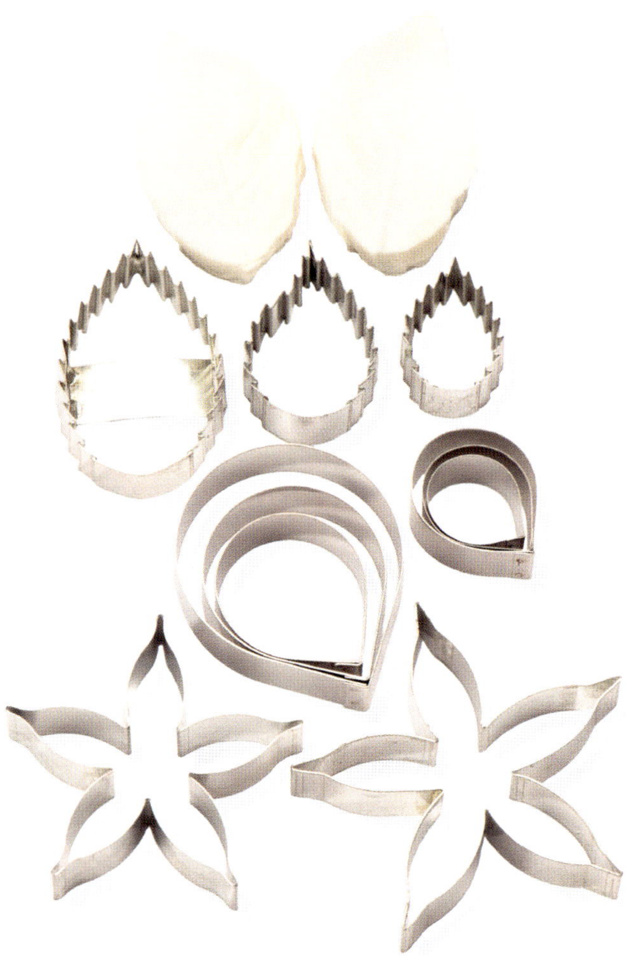

Note: Although each set of cutters and veiners are shown together to show their relative sizes, the scaling of each set may vary due to the space available.

Supplier Codes (see Page 76 for addresses):

SKGI – Squires Kitchen Great Impressions
KB – KIT BOX
FC – Fine Cut
FMM – FMM
TT – Tinkertech cutters
PME – PME Sugarcraft

Equipment - Roses

Rose leaf veiners (SKGI)
Rose leaf cutters (FC 570, 575 & 576)
Rose petal cutters (KB 0519 & 0052)
Rose calyx cutters (FC 175)

Equipment - Rose Hips

Rose leaf veiners (SKGI)
Rose leaf cutters (FC 570, 575 & 576)
5 petal calyx cutter (FC - several sizes)

Blackberry

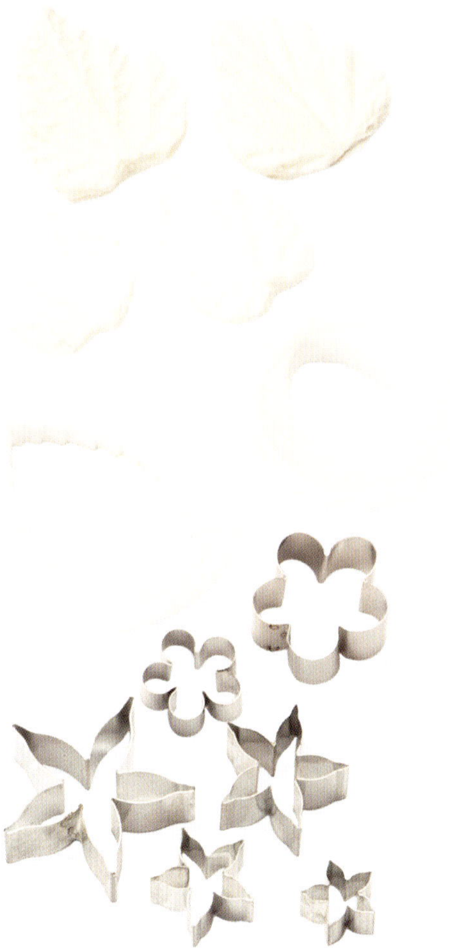

Equipment - Blackberries

Blackberry leaf veiners (SKGI)
Rose leaf cutters (FMM RL2 & RL3)
5 petal blossom cutter (KB 07 & 02)
Calyx cutters (FC 165 / set of 3)

Acorns & Oak Leaves

Equipment - Acorns

Oak Leaf veiner (SKGI)
Oak leaf cutters (FMM Oak 1,2 & 3 and FC 450 & 455)

Honeysuckle

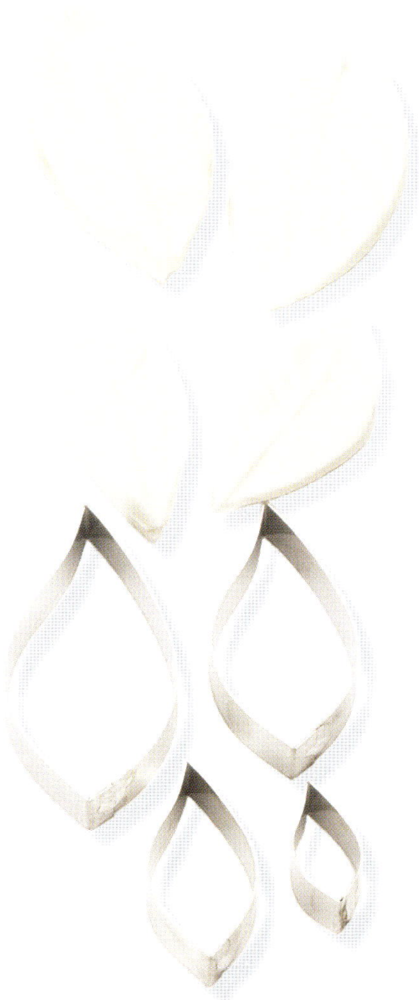

Equipment - Honeysuckle

No cutters for the flowers – just your hands.
Honeysuckle leaf veiners (SKGI)
Metal leaf cutter (FC leaf set 362)

Hypericum

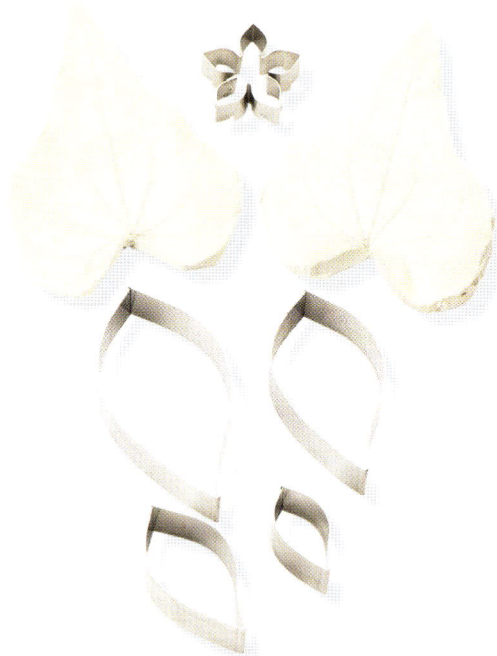

Equipment - Hypericum

5 petal calyx cutter (KB RO12)
Black bryony leaf veiner (SKGI - use the centre vein)
Metal leaf cutters (FC 362 / set of 3)

Monbretia

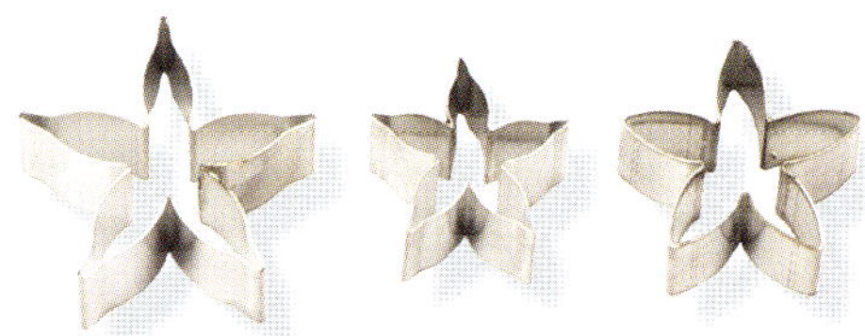

Equipment - Monbretia

5 Petal calyx cutter (FC 165 / set of 3)

Ivy

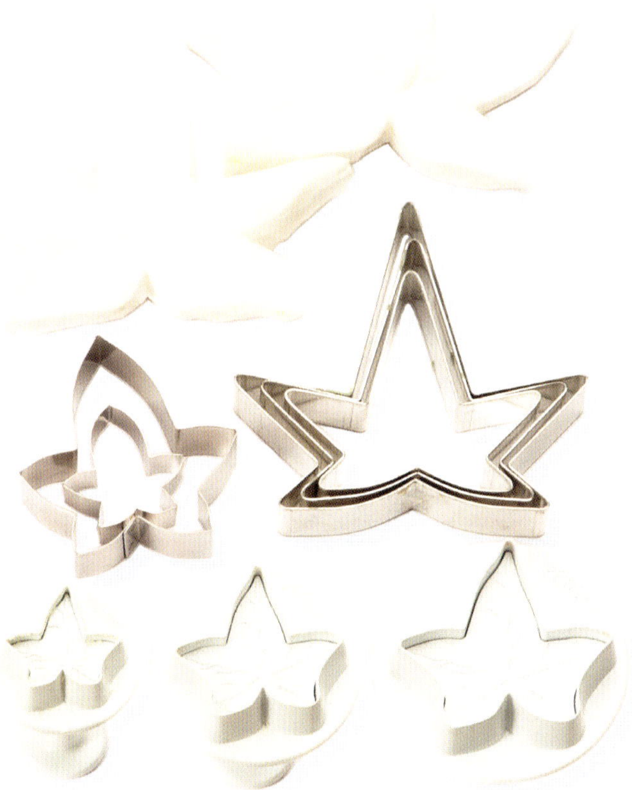

Equipment – Ivy

Birdsfoot ivy leaf veiner (SKGI)
Ivy leaf cutter KB Size 3 R034, Size 2 R033 and Size 1 R032
Ivy leaf cutters TT metal cutter set 45-60mm
Plastic cutter and veiner plunger set PME

Conkers

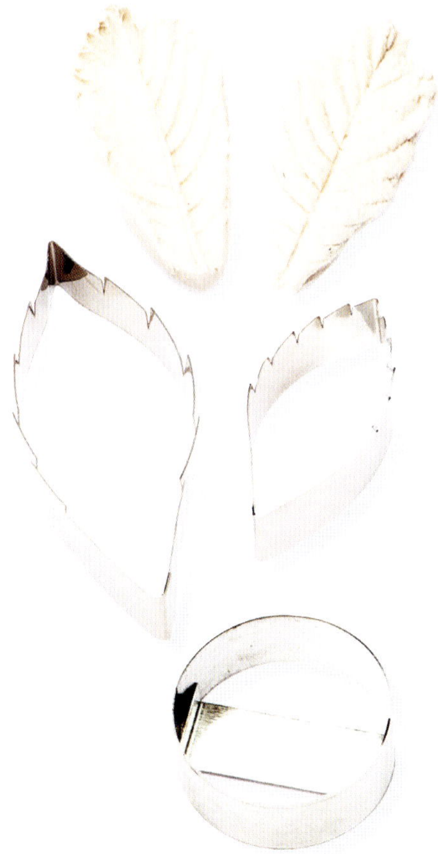

Equipment - Conkers

Cutting wheel or circle cutter FC Circle 1850
Horse chestnut leaf veiner SKGI medium
Horse chestnut leaf cutter KB set 0135

Acknowledgements

My sincere thanks to Agneta Olsson whose faith and friendship has opened up many opportunities and encouraged me to pick up the ball and run with it. To Andrew Gransden for his superb photography and design skills which have captured the purpose of this book and allowed me to show the subject in reality. His expertise and patience in enabling me to translate my vision into print is beyond value and I am hugely grateful. My thanks also to Andrew's wife Fiona, for her critical eye, understanding of the long hours and keeping us fed and watered. I am grateful also for the time given by Julie Askew, who by a fortunate meeting has allowed me access to the dimensions of an Editor's mind; and also to Carolyn Harvey for her advice, valued comment and clarity; and to all my colleagues, family and friends for their contributions in an editorial role.

I would like to thank Dyck Willis of Kit Box, Grace Clements of FMM Sugarcraft, Beverley Dutton of Squires Kitchen, David Wregg of Fine Cut Cutters and Pauline Adams of The Sugar-Mill for their generosity and support.

Close to home thank you to my sisters Jacki and Clare for their laughter, unconditional support and contribution in many ways to this book. To my sons Peter and Felix for loving me and understanding when time has been short. I am indebted also to my close friends, Judith and Doug, Lesley and John and Alastair and Carolyn who each in their own way, mean more to me and my boys than they will ever know; and to my good friend Jenny, a constant sounding board, thank you. An exceptional bunch of people. Thank you all for being in my garden.

Finally, with love to my Mother and Father Anne and Henry Reynolds, who although sadly no longer in the present, are never regarded as being in the past.

Coming next

I hope you have enjoyed this project as much as I have had pleasure in writing it. During the process I realised that there was much more I would like to teach that would not fit into this book, therefore coming soon Book 2 which will be based around a collection of Spring and Summer Flowers.

You will find details of workshops and other events on www.alyson-reynolds.com. Please don't hesitate to contact me directly to arrange a workshop or demonstration tailored to suit yourself or for a group in your area.

A note from the author

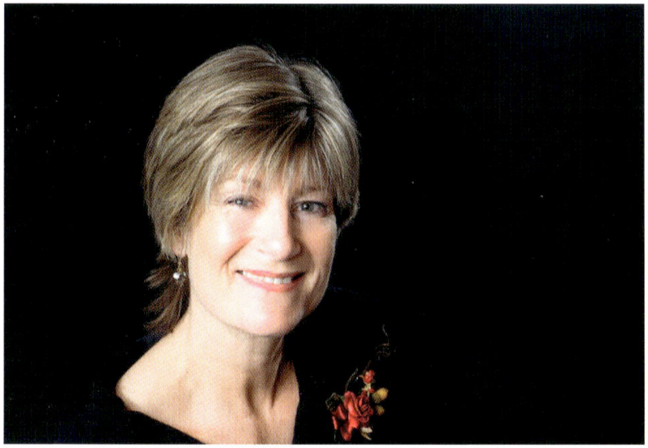

When I was 5, I wanted to drive a tractor. When I was 10, I was going to be a nurse. At 14 the world was my oyster and I could potentially be a Doctor, an Accountant, maybe even a Lawyer. By 17 my earlier aspirations had been curtailed somewhat and the suggested career paths were now of a more practical and creative nature. My thoughts ran towards training as a Plumber, an Electrician, a Builder or an Actress? "Don't be ridiculous" said my mother and with that I was sent to Secretarial College to get myself a skill ...

Thirty one years on, I believe I have achieved most of my earlier ambitions in one way or another - as well as many I never expected.

I have tended to grazed knees, fractured bones and broken hearts. I joined the Royal Air Force and became responsible for Accounts. I have two wonderful sons and have prosecuted, defended and ruled in judgement between those two parties on many occasions. I can stop a dripping tap, unblock the sink, bleed a radiator and I know where the stopcock is. I am able to efficiently change a plug, re-wire a light fitting and through trial and error (and admittedly the odd minor shock) have made friends with the fuse box. I have built a wall, a hen house and without even thinking, a home for my family. Shakespeare wrote something like "The World is a stage and we are merely players...", so if that counts, I consider myself to have an on-going 'bit' part. I have yet, however, to drive a tractor.

On leaving the RAF in 1996 whilst expecting my first son Peter, I undertook a 2 day resettlement course on Cake Decoration. Here I found out that I couldn't ice a cake to save my life, however there was potential with the flowers! I took up sugar crafting more seriously in 1998 following the birth of my second son Felix, in the hope that it would help me keep my sanity and vary the topic of conversation from 'Is he on solid's yet'?

Since then I have specialised in Weddings - making Bridal bouquets, cake decorations and many other bespoke floral arrangements. I have been invited to judge various competitions and have also had the opportunity to demonstrate and exhibit my work in the UK, USA and Europe. Most of all however, I enjoy teaching and have been fortunate to use my skills in workshops at home and abroad.

Throughout all of the above, my Secretarial training has enabled me to negotiate and administer the multitude of peaks and troughs. For this and hopefully much more to come, I have to thank my Mother.

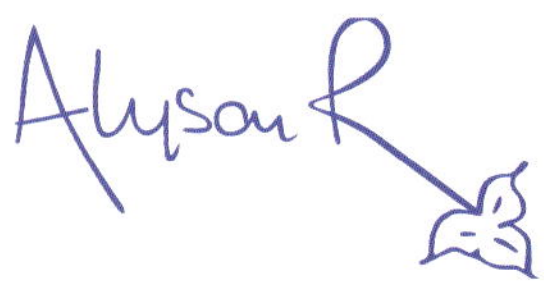

Suppliers

I would like to thank all the Suppliers listed below for their support with this project and point out that they all stock a multitude of items as well as those directly mentioned.

KIT BOX
Metal stainless steel cutters
Unit 3 Neads Court
Knowles Road
Clevedon
Somerset BS21 7XS
www.kitbox.co.uk
support@kitbox.info
01275 879030 tel/fax

Fine Cut Sugarcraft Products
Metal Tin plate cutters
Workshop 4
Old Stable Block
Holme Pierrepont Hall
Nottingham NG12 2LD
www.finecutsugarcraft.com
info@finecutsugarcraft.com
0115 9334349 tel/fax

A Piece of Cake
Flower paste, Porcelain and all equipment
18 Upper High Street
Thame
Oxon O89 3EX
www.sugaricing.com
sales@sugaricing.com
01844 213428 tel/fax

Squires Kitchen
Great Impressions veiners
The Grange
Hones Yard
Farnham
Surrey GU9 8BB
www.squires-shop.com
customer@squires-shop.com
0845 6171810 tel
0845 2255673 fax
+44(0)1252 260260 overseas

FMM Sugarcraft
Plastic cutters
Unit 7, Chancerygate Business Park
Whiteleaf Road
Hemel Hempstead
Herts HP3 9HD
www.fmmsugarcraft.com
sales@fmmsugarcraft.com
01442 292970 tel

Orchard Cake Tools
Plastic cutters
Prins Mauritslaan 76
6191 EH Beek, Netherlands
www.orchardcaketools.com
info@orchardcakeacademy.com
+31 464 362672 tel/fax

Tårtdecor Sweden AB
Everything you need
www.tartdecor.se
Utmarksvägen 18
442 39 KUNGÄLV
+46 0303 51470 tel
+46 0303 243099 fax

The Sugar Mill
Colour Dusts and Liquids
www.thesugar-mill.co.uk
01773 570737 tel